Bromle

30128 80

D0548277

The Girls
in the
Wild Fig
Tree

NICE LENG'ETE

with Elizabeth Butler-Witter

The Girls
in the
Wild Fig
Tree

How I Fought To Save Myself, My Sister
and Thousands of Girls Worldwide

WILDFIRE

First published in 2021 by LITTLE, BROWN AND COMPANY
a division of HACHETTE BOOK GROUP, INC.

First published in the UK in 2021 by
WILDFIRE
an imprint of HEADLINE PUBLISHING GROUP

1

Cataloguing in Publication Data is available from the British Library

Hardback ISBN 978 1 4722 7580 6
Trade paperback ISBN 978 1 4722 7581 3

Offset in 12/17.5 pt Adobe GaramondPro by Jouve (UK), Milton Keynes

Printed and bound in Great Britain by Clays Ltd, Elcograf S.p.A.

MIX
Paper from
responsible sources
FSC
www.fsc.org   FSC® C104740

Headline's policy is to use papers that are natural, renewable and recyclable
products and made from wood grown in well-managed forests and other
controlled sources. The logging and manufacturing processes are expected
to conform to the environmental regulations of the country of origin.

HEADLINE PUBLISHING GROUP
an Hachette UK Company
Carmelite House
50 Victoria Embankment
London EC4Y 0DZ

www.headline.co.uk
www.hachette.co.uk

To my parents: I hope I have made you proud and that the bravery and strength I saw in you, the joy, compassion, and commitment that you taught me, I have been able to share with others.

To the girls who have been mistreated and forgotten, and who dare to dream: I hope this serves as an inspiration that your dreams and hopes will always be bigger than your reality and that you can achieve anything.

To my sister, beloved family, friends, and all who have walked this journey with me: thank you.

To the girls in A Nice Place Rescue Center and Leadership Academy: you are the future!

The Girls
in the
Wild Fig
Tree

Names

When I was born, people said I had smooth skin and bright eyes. My parents gave me the nickname Karembo, meaning beautiful.

I still like to tease my older sister, Soila, that when she was born, no one called her Karembo. My mother said that when she came out, her skin was wrinkled and her head ended in a sharp point. Even those who looked with the most loving eyes had to admit that she looked a little like a conehead.

We were wanted and loved, coneheads or not. To a Maasai, no man is wealthy unless he has many cattle and many children. As soon as a baby is born, the father hosts a large party. There is tea and roasted meat for everyone, and people bring presents for the family. My father liked to show us off to his friends. He brought a coworker, a white English speaker, to my celebration.

"Isn't she a pretty one?" he said, watching me smile. "Nice baby, nice baby," he cooed.

"I like that," said my father. "We will call her Nice."

He also named me Retiti, after the oretiti tree that grows in our part of Kenya. It spreads by sending down shoots that form new trunks, and after many years, walking beneath a single tree can feel like walking through a massive grove.

Some people use oretiti bark for medicine. The wood is strong, good for making sticks to help herd animals. The tree produces figs to feed animals and people. It offers shade in a part of Kenya that is often dry and dusty. In the days before most of us converted to Christianity, people would pray under the branches of the tree and make offerings of cow or sheep blood in times of trouble. Some still pray there; the many trunks of the oretiti can feel as cool and sacred as a cathedral.

The oretiti, people say, has many branches. It is a single tree, but it can support many people.

When I was young, the children would tease me for the name. "Ret-tet-tet," they would say, like a bird drumming on a hollow log. I hated the name and I picked a new one—Nailantei—instead. It was a traditional girl's name with no special meaning; I chose it because it sounded nice.

My aunty Grace says the old name suits me better. Like the oretiti, she says, I have grown to hold many people in my arms. I have sent down roots not just in my hometown but all over the world. People depend on me, Grace says, and if I fell, many people would weep.

It is hard for me to think of myself that way—in my heart, I still feel like a simple village child—but Aunty Grace has a point. I have devoted my life to saving girls from female genital mutilation (FGM), a brutal and sometimes deadly procedure. I have traveled throughout the world, met kings and celebrities, given speeches and received awards. I have helped save thousands of girls. I am still rooted in a small Kenyan town, but I have spread my branches wide.

It is fitting that I was named for a tree because it was a tree that saved my life when I ran away from FGM. Without that tree to hide me, my family would have cut off my clitoris. I might have literally died from FGM, but even if I had survived, I would have experienced a different kind of death. I was a young girl, but after the cut I would have been considered a woman, and I would have been married to an older man. I would have dropped out of school. I would have worked myself to exhaustion every day caring for my husband and children. Instead, because of that tree, my life has branched out into something entirely different. That tree gave me my life, the one I have now, the one that my father could not have dreamed of when he held me in his arms and called me Nice.

A Maasai Girl

I grew up in Noomayianat, a Maasai village near the town of Kimana, close to the border of Kenya and Tanzania. It is an area of plains where elephants, wildebeest, and giraffes graze on grass and the occasional spindly tree. Baboons and vervet monkeys will sneak into human homes to steal sugar or honey—like us, they have sweet tooths. Where water runs, plants are thicker, and animals gather to drink and to hunt one another. Mount Kilimanjaro looms, and at the end of the day, when the sky is clearest, the sunlight glints pink off its icy summit.

My town was small then, though it has since grown much larger. It was just a couple of streets of simple one- and two-story cinder-block buildings. Perhaps five thousand people lived in the town, though many of these, my family included, lived in homes far from the city center. The Maasai own cows, sheep, and goats, so we need plenty of space for our animals to graze.

In the center of town, there was a rickety market, and on Tuesdays people would walk from miles away to display, on upturned crates, their freshly slaughtered goat and lamb, tomatoes and onions from their small gardens, and handmade traditional clothes. Back then, the route from Nairobi was unpaved, so you needed a strong backside to ride the washboarded road. When tourists came, they usually arrived on small airstrips and bypassed our town entirely. The locals got around on motorbikes or their feet. Groups of Maasai women would cross the plains carrying loads of water or firewood. Maasai men, their bright *shukas* spots of color against fading paint and dusty plants, gathered on corners or under trees.

It is a dry place, and everywhere there is dust. Great funnel-like clouds of it move through the plains. The animals and people walk past, hardly noticing.

The Maasai have lived in this area for centuries. Unlike some of our neighbors, we never hunted. We raised cows and goats and lived off their meat and milk. These are still our favorite foods. We ate very few vegetables or plants. One of my uncles brags that he has never tasted chicken.

Families lived close together in a mixture of traditional hand-built structures and more modern concrete-block homes. Traditional homes are circular structures coated with a mixture of dung and mud. Two small beds made of stretched cowhide, one for the parents, one for the children, are the only furniture. The homes are quite small and dark, little more than shelter during the night. Most of our time was spent outside.

In our towns, someone you knew was always in earshot, and children ran in and out of one another's houses, not bothering to knock. I made friends easily—I still assume I will like every new person I meet—and there was always a friendly face.

It is still my home, though there are more buildings, more people, and definitely more cars than when I was a child. I have traveled around the world, but this area, these people, call to me in a way no other place can. I love our traditions: the bright cloth of the *shukas* we wear; the many voices, each singing a slightly different tune, blending in rich harmony in our music; the generous spirit with which we share with our families and neighbors. But I want to change much about our lives: the poverty, the lack of education, and, most of all, the position of women.

Change does not mean giving up what is good in ourselves. It means keeping what is best while accepting the need to grow. We can herd cattle while carrying cell phones. We can wear traditional clothes some days and pantsuits on others. We can eat our simple meals of meat and milk and also enjoy a spicy chicken vindaloo or a cool, fresh cucumber salad. We can maintain strong family bonds while our women get educations and bring money into the family.

I am Maasai. I am part of the community, and it is part of me. My life began here, and so did my mission.

Making Mischief

$\mathbf{M}$y early childhood was one of love, safety, and happiness. The sound of my mother's voice singing a hymn. My grandmother lulling us to sleep with stories by the fire. The feel of my father's warm hand enclosing mine as we walked together. My sister, Soila, stroking my head when I woke up from a bad dream.

Maasai mothers are loving but tough, and my mother was no exception. Since I was always getting in trouble, I saw that tough side a lot.

"Let's make chapatis," I said to my younger brother one day when I was about four. Soila moved so quickly around our home, cooking and cleaning in a rhythm with my mother, that she made the work look easy. I had watched her and my mother make the soft flatbreads that Kenyans love dozens of times. How hard could it be?

We stole into the house and took a few scoops of flour, and then mixed it with runoff water from a pipe (and a lot of stray dirt).

When the dough came together, it was much redder than I had expected chapati dough to be, and it was dotted with stray stones.

"It does not look right," my brother said.

"You are just afraid to try it."

My brother was no coward, so he took a big bite. I could not let a younger brother show me up, so I took a bite too. I managed to choke a bit of the dirty paste down, but there were tears at the corners of my eyes. My stomach did not feel so good.

A bowl of precious white flour was ruined. Every inch of skin, and even our mouths, was covered in mud.

My mother's lips got thin and tight when she saw us. She put her hands on her hips. "Look at you," she said, "playing the fool with our family's food."

I hung my head at her words, but she was not finished. She gave each of us a few hard smacks on the bottom. When she was done, she sighed and told us to go wash ourselves.

That night, when she gave soft, white chapatis to my siblings, my brother and I each got a simple bowl of stew. "You have already had your bread for the day," she said. I knew from her tone of voice not to bother begging.

We never stole flour again.

My sister, Soila, did not get in that kind of trouble, at least as far as I remember. She was three years older than me, and she seemed impossibly mature, tough, and courageous.

When Maasai children are very young, an adult heats a coil of wire over a fire until it is orange and then uses it to burn a circle on the child's cheeks. Some people say the scabs from the wounds lure flies away from children's eyes; most say the circle is a special symbol to mark us as Maasai. People say that Soila was so tough she did not even cry.

"It doesn't hurt that much," the adults told me. "Thinking about it is worse than the burn."

I had heard the children screaming when the hot metal touched their cheeks, and I wanted no part of it. The first time I saw my mother heating the wire for me, I ran into the fields and hid behind some bushes. I stayed away until bedtime. My mother spanked me, but I knew it was better than being branded. I did the same thing the second time, and the spanking got a little harder. The third time, my mother made Soila hold me while she heated the wire, but I slipped away as soon as her grip loosened.

The next morning, my mother looked at me and sighed. "You know what you want, stubborn girl. Just like your daddy. No marks for you, then." I am not certain, but I think I caught just a tiny bit of a smile.

I still have no marks.

Soila could take care of our home almost as well as our mother. When I tried to wash a skirt, it would somehow end up dirtier than when I started. As for my cooking…let's just say that everyone turned to Soila when they were hungry.

When she saw my work, Soila would sigh and roll her eyes, and then she would help me straighten a wrinkled blanket so that it would dry evenly, or she would scrape the burned bits I had left in a pot. No matter how many times she taught me, my tea would be bitter, my porridge lumpy, and I would leave messy handprints on everything I touched.

"Nice," she would say, "you are completely hopeless." But her voice was not angry. She would help me redo whatever I had "helped" with and then send me out to play.

She brushed the dust from my skirt when I became unpresentable. She braided my hair and called me a tender head when I complained about the pulling. I noticed that she was always more gentle when I cried, though, no matter what names she called me.

Games and Work

The boys and girls from my town spent our days running and playing in the land surrounding the town. We did not play games like soccer and cricket. We pretended to be little adults. We took sticks to herd imaginary cattle or scare away wild animals. We jumped as high as we could, just as the young warriors, the *morans,* did, bouncing straight up to show how strong we were. We sang our own versions of adult songs. We dared one another to jump across the creek without getting wet. Unlike the other girls, I did not like to play at being a mother; fighting off lions and hyenas was a lot more interesting. When we were not making up our own games, we worked for our mothers, gathering sticks or bringing water, and we laughed together as we walked.

Some of the children liked to race, and we picked goals as we went: first to the tree, first to the termite mound (though never on top of one: you never knew what animal had moved in), first to the stream. Soila could beat all the girls and most of the boys. I would trail behind and find her leaning on a tree, pretending that she had fallen asleep waiting for me. "Move those lazy legs, girl," she would say, but she would be smiling.

My life was not that different from that of any child growing up in a rural setting; that setting just happened to be Kenya. Tourists come from all over the world to see our wildlife. Everyone has seen photos of the herds of elephants roaming in front of a single tree in a sea of grass, with Mount Kilimanjaro a beautiful backdrop. *Majestic. Wild. Magical,* they think. When foreigners visit, they gape at the giraffes, and it baffles me. They were just the animals who slowly walked away when we came too close. We would stay clear of the lions and make jokes about the warthogs, silly animals who would run and, fifty meters later, forget what they were running from. Mostly, though, the animals were background. To me, raccoons and opossums are exotic creatures; giraffes are as normal as squirrels are to North Americans and Europeans. It is beautiful here, no doubt, and I appreciate that beauty. But southern Kenya is not some wild, majestic place to me; it is my home.

Childhood was not all play. Like most Maasai women, my mother left school as a young teen when she married my father, but she valued education and made sure we attended school and did our homework. My father, who left school after he finished his elementary education, felt the same way. First my elder brother, and then Soila, went off to school. "You will get the education we did not have," my parents said. "You will be the hope of the Maasai."

I was about three when Soila began school and left me home with my mother.

When she returned home after the first day, I followed her. "What was it like? Can you read now? Will you read me a story?"

"We learned some songs. And I can write three letters," she said. "*A, B,* and *C.*"

"Show me, please," I said.

Soila picked up a stick and slowly traced the letters in the dirt.

"What do they mean?" I asked.

"They make sounds," she said. "There are more."

I nodded, and then I picked up a stick and copied her letters.

Every day after that, when she got home, I would beg her to show me what she had learned. When she was not too busy, she would teach me.

When she was gone during the day, I would imagine myself in a fancy school uniform going off each day to learn about mysterious things like letters and numbers until my mother shouted for me to pay attention.

When I daydreamed during my work, I might get yelled at by my mother or Soila...or I might get yelled at by any member of the community. A boy who disrespected an elder might get a slap from any nearby adult. A girl who stood talking with her friends instead of collecting wood might get a talking-to from her mother...or any mother who saw her loafing. I did not fight or steal or disrespect my elders, but I knew that if I did, I would get caught and punished.

My family would be watching me the most closely, and family, to the Maasai, is a much broader term than in Europe or the United States. Like all Maasai, my father was part of an age-set. When he was about twelve, the elders in his community decided it was time for him and all the boys close to his age to become men. There are no set rules for how many boys are initiated, or how often the initiation occurs. They could be as young as my father or as old as their early twenties. There could be five boys or fifty. I am not sure how many were initiated with my father, but the group must have been fairly large because every day a boy seemed to stop by to join my father for tea, and even today, men introduce themselves to me as age-mates of my father.

The boys in the age-set spent months preparing, learning from the older men how to butcher meat, use a spear, start a fire with just sticks, minister to cattle when they fell ill. The men taught the boys how to treat their wives and children. They even taught them how to kill lions, the only animals Maasai men hunted. When they had learned what the elders had to teach, the boys were circumcised together. My father was brave, so I knew he would have stood still and silent while he was circumcised. There was no anesthesia, and he was expected to hold still and stay silent. Afterward, the boys lived together in a small village of their own for a few months. There was no fence to protect them, and in my area hyenas and lions roam at night. I imagine they sat by the fire late in the evening, making jokes and talking about women to avoid thinking about the fear and the pain.

When they were all healed, the boys were initiated into manhood together and became *morans,* or young warriors. They also became lifelong friends and family. Age-mates helped one another herd cattle, loaned one another money, shared their food and sometimes even their wives. When a man visits an age-mate, he might sleep with his friend's wife (if she is willing), and because they are all tied to one another, it is not considered shameful for the woman or the men.

A man's age-mates are his brothers. When I visit home, I sometimes see men walking together, holding hands, and I think of my father and how he would walk with his friends the same way.

When my mother married my father, she became a member of his age-set. In a way, she became mother to all the group's children as well. I remember my younger brother and I walking far from home one day, pretending we were hunting lions. We stopped to rest near a stream, and both of us realized it was afternoon. Our feet were sore, we were hungry, and home was several miles away. A group of men stood talking nearby, and I recognized one from when he had shared tea with my father. My brother and I approached, heads bowed.

"Nice?" he said. "Why so far from home?"

"I am sorry. We were walking, and we are hungry."

"Yes," he laughed. "Your father tells me you are always hungry."

He gestured to the left. "Walk that way until you see my home. My wife will fill your greedy little bellies."

We thanked him and ran. My feet no longer bothered me because I knew there was food nearby.

Visiting

My grandparents on my mother's side lived fifteen kilometers from the nearest road, so we would hike through the brush to visit them.

The first visit I can remember was when I was around four years old. The journey felt endless. "Pick me up!" I whined at my mother. My little brother had a comfortable seat—he was tied to her back—but I had to walk, and my feet were sore. "You are big enough to carry yourself, Nice," she said.

Soila let me ride on her back for short bursts, but never for long. She was only seven, after all.

When I had convinced myself that we would wander in the wilderness for forty years, we arrived at a great circular fence built out of thorns and brush. It kept the livestock in (along with their flies) and other animals out. Like the people in the other small settlements we had passed on our hike, we were absolutely alone out there. I had heard stories of hyenas dragging children away in their sleep, but when I looked up at that giant fence, I knew I would be safe with my grandparents.

When we arrived at the gate of the enclosure, which was open in the daytime, my mother called out to her parents. They shouted back and then came out to greet us. My grandfather began to sing a song welcoming us, and then his oldest sons joined in. The women, led by my grandmother, started singing next. Each sang a different note, but the voices blended in a deep, joyful song I could feel vibrating in my chest.

Small homes, built by the women out of mud and dung, lined the fence in a circle, and the animals stayed in the center of the enclosure. Each home had two small rooms, one for the mother and father and the second for the children. Each room was about as wide as an adult's arm span. Each contained a tightly stretched cowhide that served as a bed. The homes were dark and cool—I have seen a toad or two take up residence inside—and mainly for sleeping. Most of our activities—washing, cooking, eating, playing—took place outdoors.

My grandfather slaughtered a goat to welcome us. Women were not welcome at the fire, but I could smell the roasting meat, and I realized that I was hungry.

We sat outside in a circle when it was time to eat.

First, my grandfather walked around our circle, carrying the goat's liver and a knife. He stopped before each of us and cut off generous slices. I closed my eyes while I chewed, losing myself in the rich flavor.

Next came the meat, which had been charred over the flames. The meat was seasoned with nothing but salt and fire, but the animal had been healthy and ate nothing but local plants, so it needed no fancy seasonings in order to taste delicious.

Finally, there was soup. We each received a small tin cup. It was a simple dish that used the rest of the animal plus wild herbs—some for flavor, some for health reasons. I didn't like the fatty, strong flavor, but I saw my mother staring at me so I drained my cup. "Drink your broth," Maasai women always tell their children, "if you want to live a long life."

The next morning, my mother, Soila, and my grandmother went to gather firewood.

Before they left, my grandmother showed me how to fill the cow's trough. Looking back, I realize that she and my mother probably wanted to walk and talk without a small, whining girl in the way, but at the time, I felt very important.

My grandmother left some porridge inside the house and told me to eat it once I had watered the cows.

When I returned to the house, I walked around the outside, looking for a door, but there wasn't one. The home had no windows either. As far as I could tell, there were no openings.

Unable to get into the home, not to mention hungry and cranky, I sat down and cried.

When the women returned, I was lying on the ground, dust clinging to the tears on my face. "There is no door!" I screamed before they could even ask me what was wrong.

My grandmother looked at me, turned sideways, and slid into the house. There was no door, but the house was not a perfect circle. The front wall extended about a foot in front of the wall behind it, giving the house the shape of a snail shell. Somehow I had missed this fact the evening before and in the morning. I was used to our home, a blend of Maasai and Western; we had mud and dung walls and a dirt floor, but we also had a wooden door and windows. After I followed my grandmother inside, she laughed and called me *emeeki,* our word for a non-Maasai.

She still embarrasses me by telling that story today. I was only four, I tell her. "Sounds like an *emeeki* excuse," she says, laughing.

Everyone in that small circle of homes was family. My grandfather had several wives, and I am not even sure how many children. When we were done with our morning chores, I watched them play. They screamed and laughed and ran, and I knew none of them. I stood behind Soila, glancing at them from behind her skirt.

At one point they started dancing and singing together. Something about their song seemed familiar, but I could not place it exactly. Then I remembered the previous day. They were singing the welcome song—sort of—and I was the one being welcomed. I ran out from behind Soila and we spent the rest of the day playing.

Every day during our visit, the younger children followed my grandfather, watching him inspect the cows, and I followed along. He was tall and carried a long walking stick with him, and he was wrapped in a traditional red *shuka*. His earlobes were long, with large holes he had made by stretching them out with larger and larger objects over the years.

As he did his work, he kept up a running monologue.

"I need to keep an eye on this cow's hoof. It might become infected where that stone lodged yesterday," he might say to himself.

"I must remind the women to repair the houses before the rains come."

"The fence is wearing down on the western side. I need to tell the children to collect brush to patch it."

At the time, I thought he was simply talking to himself, but I realize now that he was teaching his children and grandchildren how to take care of the animals and themselves.

"Come, sit with me," he said to us one day, stopping under a tree to rest.

"When I was younger," he said, "my grandfather taught me that all the cattle in the world belong to us. God gave them to the Maasai. So if you saw a cow with some *emeeki,* it was fine to take it. What do you think about that?"

No one answered. Obedient Maasai children are taught never to contradict or question an elder. But I knew that in the Bible other people owned cattle, and I knew they were not Maasai. I also knew that stealing was wrong.

My grandfather laughed. "You all know better than to steal another man's cattle."

We laughed too. Of course my grandfather would not steal.

"But my grandfather was not wrong," he said.

I wrinkled my forehead.

"You see, God did give us Maasai cattle. And he gave us the responsibility to care for them. If water or grass is scarce, we have to find it for our animals. If a mother cow needs help giving birth, we help her. And in return for our care, the cows give us what we need. At one time, we were the only herders in Kenya, maybe the world. So when we saw an *emeeki* with cattle, we knew it was stolen."

We nodded. It made sense. The Maasai were not stealing—just taking back what belonged to them.

"Always remember, children: we are people of the cattle."

My grandmother was pretty and neat, like my mother, even though she was old. At the time, I thought she was ancient, but I now realize she could not have been more than fifty.

Like any Maasai wife, she was in constant motion. She fetched wood and water. She cooked. She washed the clothes. She repaired her home. And she did so while smiling. "I have the best grandchildren in the world," she'd say.

One day Soila and I stood behind her while she made *ugali*. She had brought a pot of water to a boil over the fire.

"You should never rush it," she said, shaking in a tiny bit of cornmeal and stirring the pot. She handed the bowl of cornmeal to me.

"Do you like lumpy *ugali*, Nice?" she asked.

I shook my head.

"Smart girl. So add it bit by bit." I tilted the bowl, but just a bit. No more than a spoonful went into the pot.

She handed the spoon to Soila. "When it is finished, bring a bowl to your grandfather," she said, "and show him how you are going to be good Maasai wives someday."

After we ate—separately from my grandfather since Maasai men and women don't traditionally eat together—my grandmother asked Soila and me to sit and listen. Soila sat in front of her, her legs straight out, her *leso* (the cloth girls use to wrap themselves) tucked neatly around her legs. I slumped and wrapped my *leso* around my neck and shoulders.

My grandmother knelt down and gently straightened my legs.

"A Maasai girl always sits straight in front of an elder, and her legs must be stretched in front," she said, putting her hand atop my knee.

"And she is always modest in her dress," she said, gently taking the *leso* from my shoulders and tucking it around my legs.

"Nice, can you remember how to do this?" she asked.

I nodded. I understood the concept of sitting properly. Remembering was not the issue. Keeping myself from wriggling was.

"Do I deserve respect?" she asked.

"Of course," Soila and I said at the same time.

"Sitting this way is how I know you respect me. It makes me feel like a good grandmother. It makes me feel proud to see you do it."

Knowing that it made my grandmother feel good made behaving properly a bit easier. I still felt a dozen phantom itches and tingles whenever I tried to sit properly, but I could ignore them knowing that it brought her pride.

The next year, I visited my grandparents on my own. My mother took me there but stayed only a couple of days. My father and brothers needed her back home, and my sister, Soila, needed to stay and help.

When it was time for me to go home, my grandmother walked me. Fifteen kilometers is an easy walk for an adult Maasai, but my feet were on fire.

"I am hungry," I said. "My feet are tired."

On our walk to my grandparents', my mother had told me to stop complaining and keep walking, but grandmothers are more indulgent. "Hush, child," she said. "You will eat." It was not as if we could hop into a roadside restaurant or sleep in a motel, but there were many small villages, each with just a handful of homes, on the trail.

My grandmother knew these homes would be open to us. During dry periods, Maasai men can walk hundreds of kilometers searching for healthy grass for their cattle, and they know that, along the way, they can walk to any Maasai home and have a place to sleep. This way of living has created a culture of hospitality. My grandmother knew that a Maasai home meant shelter. As I still say today, "As long as I meet a Maasai person, I know I am home."

We passed a fence. It was shorter than my grandfather's, but still tall and sturdy enough to keep out the wild animals.

"Hello?" my grandmother said, leaning in through the gate.

Here there were only a handful of houses, and the animal pen held no more than fifty cows. A child, wearing nothing more than a baggy shirt full of holes, stared at us from the corner of a house. When she saw me looking, her head disappeared.

A woman walked toward the gate. "Welcome," she said. "My husband is not here, but you can come in."

The woman and my grandmother gave their names, their parents' names, their clans...I stopped listening quickly. I already knew how long Maasai introductions can take.

I started listening again when my grandmother asked if they had any food for her hungry granddaughter.

They had no food prepared, but they had fresh milk, and they were happy to share.

"It is cold," I whispered to my grandmother. I was used to having my milk warmed over the fire.

"Quiet," she said back to me. "It is good milk. And it is all they have."

I had not thought of that—only of my own hunger. "Thank you," I whispered to the woman.

We spent the night in their small home. They did not have much, and they were not even family, but they welcomed us as a matter of course—the Maasai take care of one another.

My grandmother was a great storyteller. She stayed at our house for a night after bringing us home. The children lay together on one mattress, listening as she told tales that had been passed down for centuries. My grandmother sang her stories, and I can remember how it felt to listen to her, even if I do not remember all the words. She made us hide our heads in fear, and she made us laugh so hard we rolled around on the ground. Some characters showed up again and again: the trickster rabbit who fooled the rest of the animals, the jealous woman, the hungry ogre, the greedy man. There was always a lesson hidden in the fun; we learned to do our work and share the little we had. After all, the bad people were always defeated. Those who were clever and persistent were rewarded.

These stories shaped who I became, as they have shaped generations of Maasai. I often think of these stories, and if I do not always remember every detail as they were told to me, the emotions of the stories nevertheless stay with me.

One story I will always remember: the story of two little boys who loved each other and were separated. The sounds of the boys crying to each other made me terribly sad, but it was a good, safe kind of sadness, for when I was done feeling sad, the loving face of my grandmother was there to comfort me.

The Boy Who Cried

There was once a man with two wives, and each wife bore him a son. When the elder son was young, his mother died, and the second wife took him into her home and raised him.

These brothers played together, slept in the same bed, and, when they were old enough, herded their father's cattle together. There was one gentle cow who was their favorite, and, as they wandered over the savanna with their herd, they would share her milk.

"Son of my father," they sang to each other as they milked the cow, "I will not drink without you."

The wife saw their affection growing. I work until I am exhausted each day caring for another woman's boy, she thought. My son should inherit the cattle.

"You are both looking ragged," she said that night as the boys were eating their evening meal. "Come to me tomorrow, my son, and I will cut your hair."

The next day, her son left the cattle with his brother and came to his mother's house, and she cut his hair with a razor. That evening, she said to her stepson, "Come to me tomorrow, and I will cut your hair as well."

The next morning, the mother dug a large hole by the head of the family bed. When the boy came to her for his haircut, she pretended to drop her razor. "Go into the hole and get my razor," she said, "and I will cut your hair."

Once the boy was in the hole, she rolled a large stone over him.

When the boy did not return to his brother, the people of the village searched for him, but he did not come.

"Son of my father, son of my father," the boy cried out, "where have you gone?"

They looked all day, but there was no answer, and in time the people gave up looking. He must have been eaten by an animal, they thought.

The people soon sought better grazing land. They burned their old village and moved on.

Weeks later, the older boy was herding cattle by himself, and he came across the old village. He sat on a stone. He remembered his brother.

"Son of my father," he sang, "I will not drink without you."

A faint voice sang back, "Son of my father, drink without me, let it nourish you. Your mother buried me in a hole."

The boy leapt to his feet, astonished. "Son of my father," he sang again, "I will not drink without you."

He heard the singing in response again, and he realized it was coming from the stone. He rolled the stone away and saw his brother.

The boy's clothes were tattered, his eyes blind in the sunlight. He had been eating dirt and was too weak to climb out of the hole.

His brother pulled him out, gave him his own clothes, and fed him fresh milk. When he was strong enough to walk, the boys went to the new village.

The mother had been selfish and jealous, so the younger boy sharpened his spear and stabbed her in revenge.

The boys lived together happily ever after.

The Cut

Just before dawn one morning when I was three or four, my mother walked me through silent darkness to a small home on the edge of our town. In the doorway, a girl of fourteen sat on a cowskin; the women stood around her in a semicircle. They sang, telling her to be strong, telling her she would soon be a woman.

I could hear the men, nearby but out of sight, singing. They had been drinking homemade beer. What we had come to see was a female matter, but the men would sing out and encourage the women, wishing strength and courage. It was a celebration for the entire community. Sometimes the voices, male and female, would call and respond to one another.

The light was still pink and faint when they began what we had come for: the cut. The girl held her lips tight and muscles stiff. She closed her eyes and swallowed hard. We all moved a little closer. An aunt knelt by one leg, her grandmother by another, and they pulled the girl's knees far apart. Her mother sat behind the girl, holding her steady. The girl leaned back. She closed her eyes. It seemed, for a moment, that nothing would happen. Everyone was still in the early morning light. Then an older woman, a midwife from a nearby town, stepped forward and slashed the girl between the legs with a razor. Blood sprayed across the woman's hands and the cowskin. She cut again and again.

"Get it all, get it by the root," the women chanted. The girl stiffened, trying not to cry out. The midwife pulled the girl's clitoris taut and cut, pulled and cut, while the girl clenched her teeth and sweated. I could hear the flesh tearing and smell the iron in the air. Blood dripped down the midwife's wrists.

Finally, she was finished. The girl's body shook, but her mother held her tightly until she was able to breathe again. The women helped her to her feet. She walked shakily into the house and collapsed on a straw mattress. I stared from the doorway, holding my mother's hand, as the girl screamed, her body convulsing from the pain.

I was quiet and still that afternoon. I did not ask question after question of Soila; I did not even complain about the work.

"What is wrong with you today?" Soila asked me.

"Is that girl going to be okay?" I asked her.

Soila stood still. "Everyone gets the cut. She will be fine."

But the girl was not fine. A few days after the ceremony, she developed a fever. In a few more days, she was dead. Someone had placed a curse on the family, people said.

The night she died, I curled up next to Soila in bed. "What if someone curses us?"

"No one is going to curse you, Nice. Now go to sleep." She rubbed my back for a few minutes, and soon her breath grew steady and her hand fell away.

I stared at the wall. I had been a bad girl lots of times. My father's first wife disliked my mother. There were plenty of people who might curse us. We were not safe.

And it hurt so much. I had seen that girl scream. I had seen her shaking and sweating. How can something good cause so much pain?

Unlike many of my childhood memories, this one I can see, when I close my eyes, in absolutely clear detail. It is one I wish I could block out.

Over the next few years, I witnessed perhaps ten cutting ceremonies. It never got easier.

My parents' faith in tradition was why my mother took me to see my first circumcision. There is a story that Maasai mothers and grandmothers tell their daughters about the origin of the cut. My mother and grandmother told it to me. Once upon a time, the story goes, the Maasai were at war with the hunters who lived alongside them. The hunters had grown greedy and lazy and stole the Maasai cattle for food, and the Maasai fought to protect what was theirs. One day a Maasai girl saw a beautiful warrior among the hunters and fell in love with him. She did not care that his people stole from hers. She did not care that he was fighting her father and brothers. All she cared about was her lust, and she slept with the warrior. When her people discovered what she had done, they wanted to make sure lust never motivated her again. They cut off her clitoris. After that, the girl stayed loyal to her people. The Maasai were so moved by her change in behavior that all Maasai women received the cut.

The cut became part of our identity as a people. Teaching your daughter about the cut was part of teaching her to be a part of the community. My mother had the cut herself. Her mother, her grandmother, and all our mothers stretching back into history had suffered through the cut. There was pain. But we were Maasai, and we bore that pain with strength. That suffering was part of being a woman and being one of our people. My mother knew about the dangers, knew about the pain, knew about the consequences for the girl, but still, she took me by the hand and walked me to the ceremony. It was who we were.

Maasai boys and girls undergo circumcision before they are considered men and women. For boys, that means removing the foreskin. It is a painful rite, but a boy loses no sexual pleasure, and there are few if any long-term side effects.

For girls, circumcision means removal of the entire exterior of the clitoris. Traditionally, girls receive no antibiotics or painkillers. If the bleeding is heavy, the midwife smears a mixture of cow fat and mud or dung on the wound to try to stop the blood. Some girls die from shock, blood loss, or infection. People make excuses—the girl was cursed, she had health problems, the family was weak—but I suspect we all know that the real cause is the cut itself.

The procedure can cause lifelong health damage: scarring, cysts, and abscesses. Sex and urination may be painful. Some women experience infertility because of recurrent infections from the cut. For women who get the cut, sex becomes at best a duty, not a pleasure; at worst, it is a painful ordeal. Childbirth becomes far more dangerous. "Circumcision" brings to mind the small snip that boys get. For women, the procedure is far more serious and far more destructive. Because it is so damaging, I prefer to call it female genital mutilation.

Even with all the harm the cut causes, for most Maasai girls, the consequences of not getting the cut are worse than the dangers. Without the cut, girls are not considered adults. They cannot marry or have children. Their families are shamed, and the girls are outcasts. My mother knew I would suffer as she had suffered if I got the cut, but she also knew that without it, I would never take my place among the Maasai.

I value tradition. I was a girl who listened to her family. But that morning, when I watched that girl writhe in pain, a tiny doubt began to grow within me. I didn't vow to forgo the cut then. To do so would have been an unthinkable step for a four-year-old girl. But I began to fear it.

As I grew, so did my doubts. I had always been a girl who got lost in her own thoughts. Too often, those thoughts were about the cut. I thought of that girl dying even though everyone had said she would be fine. With each subsequent circumcision I witnessed, with each spurt of blood, the doubt grew stronger. When I saw girls drop out of school immediately after getting the cut, that doubt spread. When I saw more girls sick or dying from "a curse," that doubt took over.

"I do not want the cut," I finally admitted to myself when I was about six. I did not plan to run away, not then. I still thought I would get the cut. After all, not getting it meant becoming an outcast, and I did not want to be alone. But I was able to admit to myself that I did not like everything about our traditions. And I daydreamed of running away the way I had run away from the metal that would scar my cheeks.

I loved my family. I loved my people. But this, I thought, was wrong. Tradition can be good. Tradition can be beautiful. But some traditions deserve to die.

A Maasai Bride

One of my uncles recently gave me a photo of my parents. They are posed stiffly in front of a plain pink photographer's background. We were not wealthy people who were able to record each detail of our lives on film, so the picture must have been taken when a photographer came to church or to my father's place of work. In the photo, my mother has neatly braided hair and a floral outfit; my father wears an impeccably pressed black suit. My mother's circular scars—the marks made by the metal coil that I had run from— are clearly visible. Neither smiles. My parents look handsome and successful, but it is not how I remember them. They were never stiff in their Sunday best.

My father always had a smile. He was a local politician, working to make the lives of the Maasai better. He took time to listen and share even with the youngest people, and he had a kind word for everyone. He kept coins in his pocket to give to children. I loved the taste of something sweet, and he would smile as he gave me a little money for candy.

My mother was always well dressed, just like in the photo. Her beautiful bright red shirt and blue skirt were always clean. She wore her hair long and had a tooth gap, considered beautiful among the Maasai. Though the picture shows her looks, it misses her gestures: her hands were always busy. The photo does not capture her feel and smell. She worked hard but kept her hair neat and her skin soft. Every evening, she would rub herself with Lady Gay lotion and dust herself with powder. If I close my eyes, I can still catch a hint of that scent.

My mother and father raised four children together: my elder brother; Soila; me; and my younger brother. My father also had two daughters and three sons with his first wife, and they lived a short walk away.

Maasai rules about marriage and sexuality are different than in the West. Monogamy is not the standard to aspire to. Maasai men usually marry multiple wives, and usually their wives live near one another in peace. Maasai women know their husbands can care for them while caring for other women as well. The Maasai do not divorce. When a man gets tired of his wife, he will not abandon her and their children so he can marry a younger woman. Family sticks together. Maybe we do not have monogamy, but we do have morality.

Things are changing, though. Many young women—myself included—do not want to be a second or third wife. Recently, an older woman told me, "You young women are so selfish—why aren't you willing to share your husbands?"

One day I came home and told my mother that the first wife had given me a chapati.

My mother grabbed me by the shoulders. "Listen to me, Nice," she said, leaning down and speaking slowly. "Never eat anything she gives you. Ever. She could poison you. It is not safe."

She also told me the first wife was lazy and unfriendly. The woman never wanted to be a politician's wife and would not serve tea to strangers or welcome them into her home. My mother claimed that the first wife fought with the neighbors and her own family and disrespected my father. I don't know how much of that was true and how much of that was rivalry, but over the years, many people have told me that the first wife was a poor match for my father.

Whatever we thought of my father's first wife, we loved our half brothers and half sisters, and my mother was just as loving and just as tough (she did not put up with any nonsense) with them as she was with us. She fed them, mended their cuts, and hugged them as if they were her own.

My mother was a schoolgirl when she met my father. Her name was Alice Mantole. She had to walk many miles to her boarding school, too far even for a Maasai to make it in one day, and she would stop at the home of the people who would become my paternal grandparents. My grandparents were not relatives or close friends of my mother's family. The reason she stopped there was simply that it was a Maasai house along her route. Welcoming other Maasai, family or not, is part of our culture.

While there are local schools in most Kenyan towns, many do not go beyond teaching the bare basics. Local schools have few teachers with far too many students. There is no money for even the basics such as pencils and paper. Because students are expected to work with their parents at home, children have little time to devote to academics, and progress is slow. Boarding schools, on the other hand, offer a place where students can devote themselves to working on academics full-time. These are not the elite, expensive institutions familiar to Westerners. Most are state-owned schools with low fees, though for poor Kenyan families the investment is still substantial. Students work in simple concrete-block buildings. They do not have air-conditioning or computers for each child. The boarding schools do, however, give students the time to learn and provide teachers to teach them. My mother and her family wanted her to get a solid education, so she had to travel for school.

Kenyan boarding schools are out of session in April, August, and December, so my mother had to make the journey six times a year, and my paternal grandmother got to know her well. My mother helped my grandmother with the cooking, and she swept the floor clean when the family was done eating. She was respectful, bowing her head to her elders the way Maasai young people are taught. When she was done helping, she would quietly study her books. She was going to be the first in her family to finish school.

"Come and visit us," my grandmother told my father, "and meet this girl."

I was not there to see them meet, of course, but I asked my mother about it one day when I was about five and "helping" her with the laundry. With Soila at school, I was lonely, and I wanted someone to talk to.

"Your grandmother asked me to wait a bit before I set off for school one morning. It was getting late. I had a long way to go. 'One more minute, one more minute,' she kept saying. Then your father walked in, and I was glad I waited. He was the most handsome man I ever saw."

I shifted and looked away. My father was handsome—everyone said so—but no one wants to hear her mother speak that way about her father. And it was hard to picture him as a young man. I could not imagine what their world was like before I came into it. I could not imagine my parents not knowing each other.

"So you got married?" I asked.

She laughed. "Well, not quite as quickly as that. You think I would run off with a man I barely knew? I stopped at his parents' home every trip to and from school. Seemed like from then on, every time he would be there."

"Then you married him," I said.

"After we talked many times. He was more than a handsome face. He was serious. He talked about how he was going to bring money to his people. He was going to make sure children went to school. He was going to change everything. But it wasn't boasting the way young men do. He had plans. He was going to carry through. When you listened to him, you wanted to help make those dreams happen."

I recognized my mother's description. That young man was my father.

"Maybe I would have married him right away, though. When I met him, I knew this was a man I could love," she said.

I asked my father about their meeting.

"My mother would not stop talking about this young girl. How serious she was. How thoughtful. How intelligent. I agreed to come when she started talking about how pretty she was. But she was right. Alice is an angel. I knew the minute I saw her."

My father's first marriage was set up by his father. His second marriage came from his heart. My mother's parents urged her to stay in school. Her parents were well-off: her father had eight wives and a huge herd of cattle. They wanted their children to have an education. But my mother knew her future lay with Paul Leng'ete Ole Nangoro.

I had always assumed that my elder brother was my father's biological child, even though he was born before their marriage. There was no reason to think otherwise. My parents' love for each other and for their children was well known. My father praised my brother for the care he took with the animals, and he looked over my brother's schoolwork with pride, just as he did with his other children.

When I was home recently, I learned that my mother was pregnant when she and my father met. Having sex before marriage is not considered shameful in the Maasai culture, though having sex before the cut is. Sometimes girls have boyfriends, and they will have sex because of the affection they feel, but more often, girls will agree to have sex because they have been taught never to say no to men. Or a girl will look down when a man approaches and say nothing, shy about talking to a man who is not in her family, and the man will take that silence as a yes. Girls are sometimes sent to live with distant relatives, and they feel they cannot reject their elders. Girls simply do not have the voice or the power to say no. Premarital sex and pregnancy at a young age were common in my mother's time, and they are still common today. In Kenya, 40 percent of girls will have a child by the time they are nineteen. In some areas of the country, the rates are even higher.

I don't know why my mother was pregnant when she met my father. All I know is that she loved my father and wanted to spend her life with him. She gave birth before their wedding.

The day before a traditional Maasai wedding, the groom brings the dowry, usually several cows, to the bride's family. Then, the next morning, the girl leaves her home and walks to the groom's. There are traditions, such as spitting milk by the girl's door, tying grass to her shoes, or giving her a baby to hold when she arrives at the man's house, and these details may change from community to community, but all Maasai weddings have one thing in common: the bride weeps.

The bride loses her family. She loses her home. She loses her friends. She's marrying a man who is older and possibly a complete stranger.

My mother chose to marry my father. She was not being sent away in exchange for cows. I don't even know if my father presented my mother's father with a dowry and, if so, how big that dowry was. But in any case, theirs was a love match, not a financial transaction.

When I wanted to find out about their marriage, I asked one of my father's age-mates, his closest friend. He smiled. "Those were two people," he said, "who fit together. It was a happy wedding."

My mother and father lived far apart, so a wedding progression was not possible. On the morning of the ceremony, my mother's family borrowed every car and motorbike they could, and everyone drove to my father's home.

My mother wore a new outfit, bright red and blue, for the ceremony. She wore a beaded necklace the size and shape of a vinyl record album around her neck and bracelets from wrist to elbow. The jewelry was yellow, red, blue, white—adding even more color. "Your mother was always beautiful," my aunty Grace tells me about the wedding, "but on that day, she shone."

My mother's family were Christian, but they chose a traditional Maasai wedding. Like any Maasai bride, my mother was blessed with milk, and straw was tied to her shoes. The smell of cooking meat filled the air.

One thing was completely untraditional: there were no tears. My mother went to my father smiling with joy.

At the ceremony, my mother walked to my father's home with her son on her back. It is a Maasai tradition, and it shows that the man is accepting not just the woman but the child as his own. My father loved my mother, so he loved her children as well. My big brother became his son that day.

A Maasai Wife

After her marriage, my mother's day began, like that of most Maasai women, before daylight. She woke up before her husband and children to get the fire started, and then she made tea the Kenyan way: strong, with lots of sugar and milk. My father was generous with the family's money—sometimes too generous, people told me later—and we often went without sugar so other families could have enough to eat. My mother made do with what she had.

After the children were awake, dressed, and fed, she milked the cows. Then she went for water. She would walk miles to get to a clean stream. She carried water—a twenty-liter barrel on her head and a five-liter jug in each hand—and sometimes a child on her back. Then she stoked the fire again and boiled water for *ugali,* or porridge.

The rest of the day was housework and cleaning clothes. She managed to keep her beautiful red shirt and blue skirt, along with the rest of our clothes, pristine. I always managed to get them dirty again right away.

When I was small, Soila helped with the laundry, but once she started school when she was around six and I was around three or four, it was my turn to work by my mother's side. The first time I helped, my mother spoke as she worked, instructing me. "First, we bring some water to boil," she said. "Go and get some more sticks."

I ran to get fuel while she laid out what we needed. While I was gone, she set out two washtubs and filled them with warm water.

"Now we wet the clothes in the first tub, and rub soap on the dirt." Many brands of Kenyan laundry soap come in bars, not powders or liquids; it is made for people who hand-wash their clothes.

"You try," my mother said, handing me a shirt and the soap bar. "Rub and rub. Put your back into it."

I rubbed the cloth with the soap and then scrubbed it against a clean stone until I could no longer see any stains. My mother looked over my shoulder and shook her head. "Again," she said.

She washed three garments while I worked on my small shirt. My fingers were wrinkled and my small hands ached.

"Good." She nodded at last. "Now rinse."

I placed the shirt in the second tub of water and rubbed and rubbed some more.

Then we wrung out the clothes and spread them out over some bushes to dry in the sun. I realized how heavy cloth could be when it was wet.

When we were finished, my hands were dry and gray. "Good, Nice," my mother said when the shirt was drying in the sun. "Now go play."

I ran off, but my mother kept working.

She chased away the omnipresent dust from the dry climate of southern Kenya by carefully sprinkling water over the dirt floor.

Our home was a blend of Maasai and Western traditions. It was larger than the traditional Maasai homes, which are used almost exclusively for sleeping or sheltering from the weather. But the walls were made of mud and dung, so constant repairs were necessary to keep the house from washing back into the soil. Unlike a traditional home, it had screened windows to let in light and air and a solid wood door to keep out flies.

When my father had guests over, as he did frequently, my mother would stop her other work to welcome them with a cup of tea. Fuel for the fire meant another long walk and another heavy load.

If she sat, it was not to rest. It was to repair our clothes or make beadwork, both for our own family and to sell. Using a sharp, dry piece of straw, a needle, or a piece of wire—whatever was handy— she would pick up beads and carefully put them on a string, and then, after a few beads, she would make a knot. She kept adding beads and knotting, slowly shaping the beads into strings and then tying the strings together to form necklaces and bracelets. The necklaces were large, colorful collars, red, yellow, orange, blue, white, green; my mother loved bright things. When she went to a wedding or birth celebration wearing a homemade necklace, she looked like a queen.

When I go home, I see women walking with massive bundles of wood tied to their backs, straps across their heads to balance the weight. They are smiling. For Maasai women, these walks are the best part of the day. Women go in groups. It is a time to sing. It is a time to share news, away from the watchful eyes of men. It is a time to tell jokes, often at their husbands' expense. Sometimes aid groups arrive in Maasai communities and build wells. When the workers return, they cannot understand why the women bypass the wells and walk long distances to streams. It is because for many Maasai women, walking is their only time for sharing, friendship, and even a touch of freedom. My parents' marriage was a good one, so my mother did not have to escape my father on her walks, but even so, she cared for her friends and welcomed that time with them.

At the end of the day, she had another meal to cook. She heated up milk—my favorite—or made a soup out of a bit of meat and some greens. Maasai men spend their days walking, looking after the animals, and talking to one another, and they expect food to be ready when they come home. They expect their wives to be home waiting, answering their calls when they enter their compound. My mother was a good wife, and I remember her smiling affectionately when my father sat down to eat. Though she did the work with pride and love, it must have been exhausting, especially with four young children around.

A good Maasai daughter helps her mother with the work. Soila was a great daughter, and I intended to be one. Once Soila started school, I tried to fill in for her. But my mother was always calling for me. "Nice, where are you?"

I would take twice as long as any other child to do the dishes. The plates would sit as the water cooled, and I would stare into space, lost in my own thoughts, rather than scrub. Housework did not interest me, so it was easy for me to lose focus and forget the task at hand. Soila says that if I have a coin in my pocket, I will give that money to someone else to do the work for me. She is right. I still hate doing the dishes.

I cannot recall my mother ever complaining. She was proud of her home. She was proud of her children, who were well groomed and always went to school. Yes, I sometimes went off into my own world, but I was also obedient and respectful; my mother would not have tolerated less. She worshipped God and made sure we went to church. We prayed and sang hymns at night. She was proud of her husband, and she wanted to be a good wife to him. She tried her best to help with his other children. She could be hard on us, but only when she had to be.

Even with all her labor, my mother found time to support other women. One day when I went with her and the other women to fetch water, she asked her friends if they had ever heard of a *chama*.

"A merry-go-round," one said.

"Yes," my mother said. "Each of us puts in some money, and we pool it together. One of us takes it home. The next meeting, another takes the money. We all share eventually."

"Who has extra money?" another friend asked.

"Nobody gives much. A few shillings. But when we put it together, it adds up."

Over the next few weeks, my mother kept bringing up the subject.

"When I try to save," my mother said, "something comes up. We need sugar. I need thread. And I am never able to save anything. When we help each other, it will be much easier."

"If we agree to do this, will you stop talking?" one of her friends finally asked.

My mother laughed. "Maybe, but I make no promises."

At the first *chama,* I served tea while the women talked. The meeting was not long—they had work to get back to—but they did take the time to visit and enjoy one another's company. At the end of their meeting, the women put their coins on the table. To me, it looked like a fortune, enough to buy all the candy in Nairobi. In reality, it probably totaled a couple of pounds. But it was enough for one of the women to buy a new cooking pot, a tea set, or enough beads to make jewelry to sell.

In a way, the *chamas* symbolized how both of my parents viewed the world. They wanted the lives of Maasai people to improve, but they did not want to give up what was special in our culture. We have always shared, always worked together instead of competing against one another, and *chamas* are a way to share in prosperity. Everyone sacrifices a little bit for her neighbor, and eventually, everyone rises together.

My mother also embraced new ways of earning money, even if it meant far more work for her. The Maasai love meat and milk; traditionally, we did not hunt or farm. My mother was the first farmer in our family, and most likely the first in several towns. She realized that, with a stream nearby, she could grow food. She ran a pipe from the stream to a small cistern lined with nylon, so there was always water for her crops.

When the garden was ready, she planted her first seeds. After the plants grew, I helped with the weeding (though I admit to accidentally picking the crops once or twice). She grew tomatoes, onions, and greens. The Buffalo Lodge, a luxury tourist resort, bought some of her produce to feed their guests. She would carry some on her back into the center of Kimana and sell it at a kiosk in the market. Some of the produce we ate—my mother was willing to break with tradition occasionally and try new things. Her food was delicious, and I learned to love vegetables from eating her tomato salad and stewed greens.

Though both of my parents helped to change Maasai culture, their marriage was a traditional one. My father was the leader, a respectful, loving leader, but very much the man in charge. My mother was the caregiver, but it was her choice. She chose to live the role of a traditional wife.

Had their marriage not been built on love, life would have been much more difficult for my mother. Her hard work could easily have been unnoticed by an ungrateful husband. She might have been beaten. Maasai men were expected to keep their wives in line, and beatings were common. Maybe she would not have been happy in her choice. Thankfully, their marriage was a good one, and I knew the safety and love of being brought up by parents who cared for each other.

Tale of the Women's Cattle

Once upon a time, women and men lived separately. The men raised cows, sheep, and goats, just as they do now.

The women's lives were easy as well. They did not have to cook pots of ugali, the cornmeal dish that every Kenyan eats, as they do now; they got their food and milk from their herds of gazelles. They did not have to walk miles to haul water or look for firewood; the zebras hauled everything they needed. They did not have to protect themselves or clean their homes and animal corrals; the elephants would stand guard at night and sweep away the dirt with their giant trunks in the morning.

Men and women were both happy in their own lives, and neither had too much work to do.

Then one day a woman noticed that her child received a very small slice of gazelle liver at their evening meal. "My children did not get their share," she said to her neighbor. "You need to give us more."

"I did not complain when your daughter drank the last of the milk," said the neighbor. "Your son does not need any more."

Soon the women were quarreling, and the rest of the women joined in. Everyone remembered a slight from a neighbor, an old wrong that had not been let go. Everyone remembered someone getting just a little bit more than they did—and forgot the times when they had taken more than their share. They fought day and night. Everyone seemed to think that her neighbor was guilty of something. No one would apologize for her own wrongdoing.

Because all the women were fighting, no one was watching the animals.

"I am tired of giving my baby's milk to these greedy women. And why should we be killed so they have meat?" said the gazelles. They wandered off.

"Why should we haul water and sticks for them when we could be growing fat eating grass?" said the zebras. They walked away.

"Why should we stand guard for women who will not keep watch themselves?" said the elephants. "I am tired of cleaning up their messes." The elephants left as well.

When the women finally looked up from their arguments, the animals were gone. They ran to chase down their herds. The gazelles and zebras were far too fast for the women. The elephants ignored the women's calls.

"Without our animals," the women said, "we will starve. What should we do?"

With their bellies empty and their children crying, the women went to the men for help, but the men had been watching the women's foolish behavior.

"You cannot be trusted to keep the cattle," the men said. "You screamed and fought while all your animals ran away."

"We are sorry," said the women. "We need your help. We will do whatever you say."

The men sat under a tree and debated for hours. Finally, they agreed to help, but only if the women followed their rules. "From now on, you will listen to the men. You will build the homes. You will fetch the wood and the water. You will care for the children. In return, we will watch the animals, and you will have enough to eat."

The women agreed. They worked from dawn to dusk, and the men cared for the animals. The work was done, and the people ate. Their children did the same, and that is how things still are today.

School

I had been watching Soila go to school for three years, and for three years I had begged her to teach me what she knew. Finally, just before I turned six, I was ready for nursery school (what Americans call kindergarten). I felt like a real grown-up.

On the first day of school, my mother set out my uniform for me and told me to go wash. When I came back, she inspected my nails and behind my ears and told me to wash again. No one would say she sent her children to school dirty.

The uniform was a simple dress with a wide collar, a hand-me-down from Soila. The cloth was a bit thin but pristinely clean from my mother's attention.

Our neighbor Buya yelled from outside, "Is the scholar ready for her first day?"

It is not unusual for Maasai children to walk several miles each way to get to class. Because Soila had moved on to a school for older children, Buya, a boy a year older and a head taller than me, would make sure I got there safely.

On the way to school, he shook his head. "It is a shame about your teacher," he said.

"My teacher?"

"She beats her students hard. Last year she broke a girl's legs."

I stopped walking and swallowed hard. "Really?"

He nodded. "You better watch yourself."

I did not speak much on the rest of the walk, so Buya talked about himself. I learned that he was going to own a thousand cows and have a dozen wives. He would have so many children they could form an army. He was going to own a car and a television. He might even be president of Kenya, but only if he had the time.

When I saw the school, I stopped walking. I thought about that girl with the broken legs.

"Nice, are you coming?" Buya asked when he realized I had stopped following.

"I am scared," I whispered.

Buya laughed. "Nice, I was joking. Your teacher is great. You have to do something really bad to get a whipping. You will be fine."

I hesitated.

Buya walked back and leaned down. "Nice," he said, "I did not mean to scare you. You will love school."

Buya was right about that last part. I cannot remember my teacher's name or where she came from. I do not even remember what she looked like or what she wore. But I remember how she smiled at each child and somehow knew each of our names.

That first day, my teacher wrote the first few letters of the alphabet on the board. "Would anyone like to try?" she asked, and I quickly threw up my hand.

I copied her letters perfectly. Soila had been a good teacher.

"Very good, Nice," she said. "You write beautifully."

I looked down to hide my giant smile.

My teacher seemed miraculous. She could speak our native Maa and Swahili, and she knew a bit of English as well. She knew counting, colors, geography, and even more songs than my mother. I fell a little bit in love with her. In my wildest daydreams, I imagined that I could be a teacher someday.

After our lessons were done, Buya met me by the classroom door.

"Did she break any bones?" he asked me, laughing.

I rolled my eyes. I had learned not only my lessons that day; I'd also learned a bit about taking Buya too seriously.

The school gave each student a big plate of beans and maize to take home for lunch. We had to cross a river. I remember it as a huge, rushing torrent, though it was probably just a small creek. "I am scared," I said to Buya.

"Give me your things, and I will carry them across, then I will come back for you."

He crossed with our things, but he was in no hurry to get me.

"Mm," he said, lifting our plates to his face. "This smells good."

"Come get me!" I screamed.

"I think I will take a little break over here," he said.

He sat down and ate his lunch.

"I am still hungry," he said, and began eating my food as well.

I stomped and cried while he laughed and ate. Eventually, he came back for me, but I was hungry.

The next day, he again told me to give him my things. "You are going to eat my lunch!" I cried.

"If you like, I could just leave you here."

I wanted my lunch, but I wanted to get home even more. I sat on the ground and cried. Eventually, he brought me back.

He kept up the same trick for weeks.

If I tried to grab a few bites of my food as we walked, I could not keep up with his pace.

If I asked him to stop by the river so we could eat together, he'd say, "No, Nice, let's cross first. I will not eat your food this time." I gave him things to carry, even though I did not trust him.

"I meant," he said as he sat laughing and eating my lunch on the other side of the river, "maybe I will not eat it next time."

Whatever I tried, in the end I would be crying in the dirt, and he would gorge himself on two lunches.

Until one day my grandmother, my father's mother, came by and saw me in tears. "What is wrong?" she said.

When I told her the story, she walked across the river. Her fists were clenched and her jaw was tight. "You think you are a big man? Stealing from a little girl?"

Buya bowed his head to my grandmother. "I am so sorry. I was joking. I will not do it again."

"Bend over," my grandmother said.

Buya turned around and said nothing. She did not hit him hard, just enough to embarrass him, but later that night, my father and Buya's spoke at our home for over an hour. At first, Buya's father was screaming. The two quieted down eventually, but when Buya's father left, he was not smiling. I did not mind the fighting because Buya never ate my lunch again.

He is now a responsible man with two wives, ten children, and many cattle, and we have become friends over the years, but he has still never apologized for stealing my food.

It is common for Maasai parents to expect their children to work, which might mean herding cattle, taking care of younger siblings, or gathering firewood and water. Schoolwork is treated as a distraction from more important tasks. Not in my family. We had to help with the washing up and the sweeping, but school was our most important work.

Soila was a few years ahead of me, so she could help me with my schoolwork at first, but I quickly passed her. My parents did not have to urge me to do well, especially with reading (math was a slightly different story). As soon as I learned to read, I would borrow any book I could get my hands on. There was no library, but there were still some books around and my teachers and our neighbors had a few. I was disappointed that there were not more books to choose from, but I was grateful for the few I could find. I had always loved stories, but they had been the ones told to me before bedtime or sung by women while they worked. Now I could have a story anytime, even, much to the annoyance of my mother and Soila, when I was supposed to be doing chores.

One day after school, I sat reading, as usual, under the shade of a tree. Soila stood nearby, talking with a group of older girls.

Four boys walked up and surrounded me in a semicircle.

"What are you reading?"

I showed them the cover and went back to my story. The boys remained standing around me. I ignored them and kept reading.

"Too good to tell me?"

"What? No. It's just a book."

"You think you are smarter than us? Because you like books?"

One boy squatted down next to me, his face near mine. His breath was hot and smelled, as though he needed to brush his teeth.

"Maybe you forgot you are just a stupid girl."

I stood up. So did he. I glanced around, but no one seemed to be looking our way. His friends stepped closer.

But before anyone touched me, Soila was there.

She stood close to the lead boy. "Meet me later," she said. She walked away without waiting for an answer.

"Oh, Nice knows we were just kidding," the boy said, laughing. "Nobody was going to hurt you, were they, Nice?" I noticed that he was looking at Soila as he spoke.

They did not bother me again.

Soila never seemed to be watching me, but when trouble started, she would be there. I knew I was safe. At night, we slept beside each other. The sound of Soila's breathing beside me was the sound of home.

Fortunately, I did not need my grandmother or Soila to help often, and I quickly adjusted to school. I became friends with most of my classmates. I have always loved people, and school meant having your friends around all the time.

Things should have felt perfect. I was happy. But there was a tiny bit of doubt and pain growing inside me each day. It had begun the morning my mother took me to see my first cut. Each day in school, that doubt grew stronger.

Many of the girls I grew up with attended school with me. One by one, their older sisters started to disappear. When they got the cut, the girls might come back to school for a few weeks, but one day they stopped coming. By the time primary school ended, when children are about fourteen, no Maasai girls were left. Aside from my teachers, I did not know any women who had attended high school.

I knew that what was happening to the older sisters was going to happen to me and my classmates. I was good at school. Working at reading and writing was not a chore. Was I supposed to just give that up? I thought about all the times my parents told me that education was the future of the Maasai. If that was true, how did getting the cut make sense? If school was so important, how could something that ended school be good?

I was still a child, and children accept that their parents are making the right decisions. As a child grows, she starts to question, though, and school was making me begin that questioning young. That questioning hurt.

I thought then, and I still think, that I had two of the best parents a child could hope for. But I started to consider that maybe they were not perfect in every way. Maybe the cut was not the best thing for me. Maybe there was another way.

Maasai Boyhood

On school holidays, I was my father's shadow. By the time I was six or seven, I could—barely—keep up with his long stride. I did not follow him in order to get coins for the candy I loved, or at least that is not the only reason. I followed him because I loved to watch the way he talked to people, and I loved the way they looked at him. Everyone would stop what they were doing and say hello. I wanted to be just like him. If Soila was my mother's, I was my father's.

Even better, when he was not meeting with people, he made time for me. On our walks, I learned who he was and how he thought. Maasai men do not often spend time with young children, even their own. Childcare is considered women's work exclusively. I felt special because my father did not chase me away; he seemed to actually want to speak with me.

So much of what I became comes from my father. If I was a shadow of him when I was little, I am still a shadow of him today. My work is different in the details, but I like to think of it as a continuation of what he started.

*   *   *

"Why didn't you finish school?" I asked him one day.

He sighed. "I wanted to, but we did not have the money."

"Were you poor?"

"It was not easy for my father. Sometimes I did not have food to eat. You know my friend Risie?"

Of course I did. He was an age-mate of my father's and he came to our house often.

"Many days, the only food I had was at his home."

"Were they rich?"

"Risie's family?" He laughed. "No, Nice, not at all. But his mother would make a little extra *ugali* to stretch out what they had."

When I visited home recently, Risie stopped by to check on me, and I asked him about his and my father's childhood.

"Your grandfather was a healer," he said. "He took care of people."

"Like father," I said.

"Oh yes. He would find the right herbs if you were sick. If you fought with a neighbor or lost a cow, he would cast the stones to help you find a solution to your problems."

"A traditional doctor," I said. "He must have known every plant."

"Yes, he did, and he knew more. He was like a psychologist. A mediator too. Maybe a bit psychic. It was good work. He helped people. But then those people did not have much to pay him."

If he had done the same work as a big-city doctor, I thought, *he could have grown rich.*

"Most of the time, your father had no shoes," Risie said. "His feet were as tough as a rubber tire. I never thought he would grow up to be an important man."

It did not surprise me that my father went hungry. For many Maasai, then and now, poverty was a way of life. But it has not always been this way. For centuries, the Maasai were the kings of the Great Rift Valley. We raised cattle. Men became *morans,* warriors who protected our people and our animals, before settling down to become fathers and elders. They were tall and handsome. Women were strong, building their houses with their own hands and taking care of their families. Our community was healthy, and we were bonded by our traditions: through clothing, through food, through music, and, for girls, through the cut.

Then came colonialism, disease, and drought. By the nineteenth century, we had lost much of our territory. Nairobi became the capital of modern Kenya. "Nairobi" is the Maasai word for cool water, but it is not our city. We are one of forty-two tribes officially recognized by the Kenyan government. The Kikuyu are the largest group, and they often dominate our government. The Maasai have had few voices speaking for us. With less land, we had to settle down rather than herd. We began eating corn and rice rather than meat and milk. We began living in dusty cities rather than quiet villages. Ranch owners and tour operators grew rich on the land and animals that had once sustained us. Meanwhile, the Maasai grew poor.

A tourist visiting Kenya today might see men in traditional Maasai clothing standing by the side of the road, drumming up business for souvenir shops and tour companies. It is honest work, and many of them are good at it. But it also makes me sad to see the descendants of men who roamed throughout Kenya, strong warriors who controlled hundreds of square kilometers of land, standing by the side of the road to advertise trinkets.

But it does not just make me sad; it strengthens my resolve. My parents believed education could lead the Maasai out of poverty. So do I.

Parks

One day, as my father and I were walking, I was telling him about a story our teacher had read to us in school, and I stopped. I thought about all the school my father had missed. *When he dropped out, I wondered, did he cry for days? Did he have to look away when he saw other children in their uniforms?*

"I am sorry you could not finish school, Father," I said. I knew how proud he was of his children's work, and how he wanted each of us to graduate.

"No need for that," he said. "I probably would have left school anyway."

I could not think of anything to say. My father was not making sense. Why would anyone leave school if they had a choice?

"I would see the tourists driving to the game reserves," he said. "Soft hands, nice clothes. And the people driving them looked almost as fat and happy. You would never see Maasai driving those vans."

"You wanted to drive the van?" I asked. I knew my father's first job was with the Kenya Wildlife Service (KWS), as a game warden.

"No, Nice, not that. What I wanted was for things to change."

"You wanted the rich people to go away?"

"Not at all. I wanted the Maasai to have just a little of what those people had. And I guess I did want Maasai to be the ones driving the vans. This is our land. Why did we have to struggle while people came and grew rich from it? The way things were just seemed so unfair."

A lot of people agreed with my father. The Maasai and the KWS have not always had an easy relationship. Many Maasai want to graze their cattle on land that historically belonged to them. When the British established the Amboseli and Maasai Mara preserves during colonial rule, they did not consult the people who lived there. To the British, our people and our cattle were nuisances in the way of the wildlife. That our domesticated animals had grazed alongside the wild animals for centuries, that we knew how to manage the land and keep it healthy, did not matter.

Some Maasai would rebel, tearing down fences so their cattle could graze. Sometimes they would even kill lions. I was speaking to an older relative recently, and he told me that, in his youth, he had poisoned lions during a dispute with the KWS. He was not proud of killing the animals, but he was proud that he had taken a stand. The Maasai do not generally kill wildlife; we respect animals and live alongside them. Unlike other ethnic groups who lived near us, the Maasai did not hunt for food. But this man and many others resented being treated as less valuable than animals.

By my father's time, the parks were in Kenyan hands, and there was even some discussion of putting a large park near our home, Amboseli, under Maasai management. But old wounds festered. The parks benefited rich foreigners, and the Maasai stood outside, receiving nothing, gazing at the rich grazing lands that had been stolen from us. Even today at the Maasai Mara preserve, there is an "animal jail" where cattle caught grazing on parkland are herded, and the Maasai cannot take back their animals until they have paid a fine. Park rangers enforce the rules; the Maasai look for ways to get around them. Generally, there is peace, but also plenty of grumbling and resentment.

"I applied to the KWS," my father told me that day as we walked.

"So you could take care of me," I said. We were not wealthy. But I had never gone without shoes. I did not have to ask a friend's mother to feed me. Some nights we might have nothing but a bowl of porridge, or *ugali,* but our bellies were full.

"You know you were not born back then, right?"

"I know," I said, looking down and biting my lip. When you are a child, it is hard to remember that you were not always the center of your parents' universe.

"I did want to take care of my children," he said gently. "You are right about that. But that is not the main reason I applied. It felt like the parks were not ours. Like we were pushed out. I wanted things to be different. I wanted to have a voice."

Sometimes Westerners and Kenyans from Nairobi who worked for the parks would call meetings with local leaders, and they would read orders about keeping cattle off protected areas, about rerouting water, about rebuilding eroded land. Scientists gave lectures about balancing the ecosystem to people who had controlled that very ecosystem successfully for centuries. They did not understand why the Maasai would ignore their orders or, often, not attend the meetings.

My father attended one of those meetings shortly after he began his KWS job.

"There was one scientist," he told me as we walked, "who named every elephant in the park. Could tell you their parents, grandparents, where they liked to graze, and their favorite water holes. I asked her to name five elders at the meeting. She could not name any."

My father shook his head. "And yet she wondered why the people would not listen."

He started asking his colleagues questions: Who is agreeing to meet with us? Who is staying home? How are they acting at the meeting? How are we acting? Is our approach working?

"You see, Nice," he told me, "when you ask people questions, it is not always about finding the answers. Sometimes it is about getting the people you are asking to think."

He questioned them until they realized their relationship with the Maasai was not productive. Only then were they ready for my father to explain our culture. When you call quick meetings and dictate solutions, the Maasai will not listen, my father explained. That is not how they talk to one another. Invite the people in, he told his colleagues, offer them food and tea, and find out what they are thinking. The Maasai would never invite someone somewhere without offering something to eat and drink. The Maasai come to solutions as a group. "How do you expect people to support rules they have no say in?" my father wanted to know. "How do you expect them to cooperate if you do not respect their traditions? It feels as if you know the personalities of the animals far better than you know the local people. You treat them like nuisances. If the Maasai are not respected, they are not going to be on your side."

This was not the way city people were used to doing business. They wanted meetings to be quick. The Maasai were used to every voice—at least every male voice—being heard. Any decision required a long discussion. Each person would give a little and receive a little in return. Arriving at a decision might take longer, but, once that decision was made, people were likely to abide by it. Peace was likely to stick.

My father was not just asking questions of the KWS. He spoke to the Maasai.

What do we need from the parks? What do we need to do to get what we want? How do the parks people behave with each other when we are not there? How do the city people think? How do they usually act?

The elders realized that the parks people did not mean to show disrespect by rushing meetings and offering nothing to eat. That is how they always behaved. Some of the elders had been to Nairobi. They had seen how people passed one another in the streets, not even making eye contact. They knew how store clerks shouted "Next!" instead of making conversation. If the behavior of the parks people was rude, it was not personal. All the elders had to do was look at the way people in Nairobi treated one another.

The Maasai learned to give as well, overlooking the quick meetings and shouted orders.

"It took a while," my father said, "but the KWS changed a bit. They listened more, spoke less. And our elders learned to be a little more understanding."

Once they realized that my father knew how to change people's minds, scientists and government officials trusted him to help them get things done. At the time, I assumed that my father was a hero who changed everything about the parks. I still think he is a hero, but I now know he was one of many Kenyans reforming the way the KWS worked. With his help, the parks became a little more friendly to the Maasai, and the Maasai began to resent the parks a little less. The parks were still a source of tension, but the Maasai began to see the benefits as well. They could be guides, sell crafts at park entrances, and even run small hotels nearby. The scientists learned that, like the elephants, the local humans had names. My father did not start a revolution, but he did his part.

Listening to my father taught me how to create change. When I work, I never go into a town shouting orders. I listen. I learn. I ask questions not only so I can better develop a plan of action but also so the people themselves can examine how they live. Sometimes a stranger asking you why you do something a particular way is an opportunity to realize that you need to do things differently.

Leadership

By the time I was following my father around, he no longer worked for the KWS. He was a politician.

"Why did you leave?" I asked him one day.

"I had earned us a bit more respect. It was all I could do in that job."

I smiled. "Everyone respects my father."

"Not exactly everyone," he said, "but you are a good girl to think so." He patted me on the head. "I left because I wanted more. If I was going to make a bigger difference, I would have to have a bigger role."

Most Maasai hold land through group ranches. These are large parcels of land on which any member of the group is free to live and raise his cattle. It is similar to the system the Maasai had in pre-British days, when clans would share large areas of land, although the group ranches are smaller in scale. A few dozen families live on each group ranch, and each has a vote in the ranch's leadership. The head of the ranch makes decisions about conservation and development, stays in contact with the Kenyan government, and resolves disputes.

The group ranch makes money by leasing some of its land to tourist businesses. Ranch leadership handed out the money to the people, who spent most of it as soon as it came in. My father realized that the way to build wealth and enrich the group long-term was through education and economic development. Motorbikes and telephones were nice, but my father felt that building up the next generation would lead to better lives for all of us in the end. He wanted to become a ranch leader and invest in the future.

My father walked or rode on his bike to visit every family on the group ranch. Just as he had at the KWS, he began by asking questions: What do we want for our people? How can we make our visions come true? What is happening to the money we take in? How can we make our lives better?

Slowly, with each conversation, people came around to his way of thinking. I was not there to see it happen, but the way my father described it, he had exactly the same conversations that I witnessed him having when I followed him on his rounds.

My father was elected leader, and with his new power, he convinced the local game lodges to hire our young people. He saw how my mother made money through farming, so he allocated two acres of arable land to each member of the group ranch for growing crops. We prefer goat meat, he said to me, but the tourists love their tomatoes. Growing locally puts their money into the pockets of our families. The Maasai started profiting, at least a bit, from the tourists.

"What if we owned the reserve?" my father asked me one day as we walked.

As much as I loved and respected my father, even I knew that was ridiculous. The government was not going to give Amboseli, the nearest park, to us. But I had been taught not to contradict my parents, and I said nothing.

"Game preserves do not have to be something that hurts us. If we control the preserve, we control the money," he said. I looked at my father. He was staring off at the horizon, not looking at me as he talked. I realized he was daydreaming, just as I did.

"There is that place by the river with the hippos..."

He spoke to all the families on the ranches and approached the local and national governments. I had not been able to watch him campaign for group ranch leader, but I watched him make his day-dream of a Maasai park a reality. When the other men did not object to a curious little girl watching, I listened to their conversations. If I stayed quiet, I learned that most of them did not seem to notice I was there.

He also spoke to government officials to get the necessary permissions, and to foreigners who were looking to make donations. A British man from an NGO stopped by our home one day. "I will make tea," I said to my mother. "You keep working." I wanted to be a good, helpful daughter, of course, but more importantly, I wanted to hear my father speak with a foreigner.

My father left school when he was young, and I was just a seven-year-old child, so neither of us could understand more than a few words of English. Fortunately, the man had brought a translator.

"Which parks have you visited?" my father asked. He nodded as the man spoke about the animals he had seen. "We also like to watch the hippos," my father said. "Carefully, of course. They can be dangerous."

The man asked questions: Would we allow livestock to graze on the land? What park infrastructure did we envision? How would that infrastructure affect the plants and animals in the park? How would we protect the animals? Did we plan any transportation improvements? How would we attract foreign tourists?

It was starting to get dark, and he and my father continued to speak. I was beginning to get hungry and realized that our usual time to eat had come and gone.

"What safeguards are going to be in place to make sure the money gets back to the community?" the man asked.

"This pr-pr-project," my father said, not able to get the words out, "will be o-o-owned..."

He stopped speaking for a moment. He closed his eyes and took a couple of breaths. "Forgive me," he said. "I have what people call a heavy tongue. When I am tired or have not eaten, it just sits in my mouth and will not let me get the words out."

The project, he explained, would be owned and run by the community itself. Profits, if any, would be earmarked for education expenses. The park would hire an accountant to make sure the money was handled properly, and members of the community would be free to examine the books.

Heavy tongue or not, my father convinced the man. That Western NGO gave money to help get the game preserve started.

The Lion Hunters

Some Maasai boys still hunted lions as part of their initiation as warriors. While it is true that the Maasai did not generally hunt wildlife, just this once in his life, a young man killed to prove his bravery. A boy who killed a lion would be famous—a boy who girls wanted to marry and men admired. In the past, when we were the only people here, killing them made sense. Too many lions meant not enough prey. They would grow thin and unhealthy, and then they would hunt our cattle.

With more development and people, though, the lions had grown scarce, and we were more of a threat to them than they were to us. The Maasai decided to stop hunting lions as part of the initiation to manhood. Instead, the young men seeking to become *morans* were expected to compete against one another in athletic competitions—throwing spears, jumping, running—to prove that they were strong and ready.

Not everyone abided by the changes: some boys wanted to prove their manhood the way their fathers and grandfathers had. A group of older men discovered that some boys had been hunting lions, so they brought the boys to my father. He could have turned them in to the authorities. Instead, he used the opportunity to change our culture from within.

They were strong boys, and proud, but they respected my father and bowed their heads to him.

He touched the tops of their heads. It is a gesture of protection and affection from an elder. The boys looked at one another, confused. They expected to be screamed at, not accepted.

"Why did you do this?" my father asked quietly.

The boys shrugged. Maybe they resented the game reserves and the rich foreigners who loved them. Maybe they wanted to become brave young warriors. Maybe they wanted to sustain our traditions and prove themselves worthy. Maybe, like young men anywhere, they were bored and wanted to flout the rules.

Whatever their reasons, they were embarrassed to have been caught and did not know how to explain themselves to an older man. They knew they might face jail time or fines larger than all the money they had ever earned.

"These parks, these lions, belong to us," my father said.

The boys said nothing. My father could see that they did not believe him. It is hard to see the game lodges full of fancy swimming pools and tents with Egyptian-cotton sheets and believe the parks are for you.

The boldest of the boys nodded. "It is my fault. I killed the lion. Punish me."

"If we are going to run this park, we are going to need men who know the area. You are good hunters."

The boys seemed confused. "We cannot hunt in a park."

"But you know the animals. You know where they gather. You have been spotting them since you were babies. You know how to keep yourselves safe."

"Yes," they said hesitantly.

One bragged, "I can spot a cheetah the guides drive right past."

"Exactly," said my father. "So stop killing and work for us."

The boys became some of the first park employees: game scouts to guide park visitors. They made a steady income, and people respected them for their knowledge. This park was not a source of resentment; it was a source of pride. Those young *morans* became enthusiastic supporters of the reserve. Not only did they never kill again, but they protected the animals. It was not long before the park was earning money as foreigners came flowing in. The park got donations from all over the world, and visitors as well. At its peak, the preserve had its own airstrip.

The money was used to give children the education my father was never able to get for himself. He sent promising young people, boys and girls, to boarding school and even college. He made sure that all children had uniforms, books, and school supplies. He worked with the government, with local and foreign charities, with local preachers and foreign missionaries, with game lodges…anyone, really, who could help his people.

A Hole in His Pocket

My father spent his own money on whoever needed it. He bought clothes for the elderly. He made sure the mentally disabled man who begged for meals from the families in town had shoes. He carried coins to give to children. It was as if he had a hole in his pocket; the money never stayed there.

An old man lived in our town. He had been injured and could no longer walk. His children and grandchildren brought him out of the house every morning and set him on a blanket in the shade of a tree. The women brought him food and water. When he needed to use the bathroom, his boys carried him there. When the children he raised came to pick him up, he would turn his head away, pretending he was not being carried like a child. When he wanted something, he would shout. But in a busy town, he was not always heard. He spent a lot of time alone.

"My doctor said I need a wheelchair, but I am not sure," he said to my father.

"You do not want one?" my father asked.

The man shrugged. "So much money. I cannot ask my children for that."

My father went around the community, collecting a few coins here and there. He contributed more than a few himself. It did not take long before that old man was wheeling himself around his compound, still yelling his orders, but now doing it with a smile.

Other people in my family were able to buy motorbikes or even cars, but my father kept the old bicycle he had always campaigned on. When we went to see the hippos at the game reserve, my uncle drove us in his car. We never told my mother how he lost control and almost drove us straight into the river.

Not that my father did not take care of us. He did.

My father's work often took him to Nairobi, and when he returned home, we would yell, "What did you bring? What did you bring?"

I remember one day, not long after he founded the game preserve, when we welcomed him home from a trip. I am not sure exactly how long he was gone. It was probably no more than a week, but it felt like months. All four of us children hugged him, and after he managed to pry us off, he opened his shopping bag and produced his gifts: flour, oil, beans. We would have real chapatis, not the mud version, for dinner.

Then he stopped. I could tell something was still weighing down the bag.

"The worst thing about Nairobi is missing you," he told us. "But the best thing"—he produced four jawbreakers from the bag—"is thinking about how happy you will be when I get home."

I loved anything sweet, especially a nice hard jawbreaker I could nurse for hours. Having my father home was better than sweets, of course, but sweets did have a way of making things better.

He never grew rich, but we never went shoeless and hungry as he had. We had good food, a solid house, and clean clothes. At Christmas, we always had new clothes and small presents. Most importantly, all his children went to school.

He would also bring gifts for his first wife and their children. Though theirs was not a union based on love, he always provided for her and their kids. It did not matter that he lived with my mother. It did not matter that he and his first wife always argued. His first wife would always be his responsibility, and my father never neglected his duties. And whatever he felt about her, he loved the children they had together and doted on them the same way he doted on us.

Eventually, my father was elected as the head of five group ranches. He knew everyone, from members of parliament to the children playing in the road. When I go to those ranches today, people stop me to tell me stories.

"He sent my son to school."

"He got me my first job."

"He saw I didn't have a school uniform and he found one for me."

A boy in town was failing his math courses. His parents had not been to school themselves, so beyond telling him to study, there was not much they could do to help. My father knew of a boy who was good at math, and he arranged for the two to live together.

The two boys studied together, and the parents made sure they worked hard. The parents did not hesitate to use the switch when their son did not concentrate. He studied, and with someone alongside him who understood the subject, he started to learn.

"Without your father's help," that boy, now a man who owns a successful business, told me, "I might not have graduated. I could not sit for a month after they took the switch to my behind, but I graduated."

Even when I go home today, some people say that my father gave too much to others, that the family should have had more. As I said, we often did not have sugar for our tea. People say he was too busy helping the community. He should have acquired more cattle. He should have acquired more wives. I do not agree. We had all we needed. We were always loved. When we followed him, he did not shoo us away as many fathers did. As long as we did not interrupt, he let us sit quietly and see how the adults did business. And when he was home, he was full of love and praise for us all. It is wrong to say he had a hole in his pocket. His money never just disappeared. It went to build a better life for people—his children included. When people say that we are just alike, as they often do, I take it as the highest compliment.

The End

In my mind, going to see the cut that morning long ago with my mother was the beginning of the end of my childhood. It does not make sense chronologically; I had several happy years after I first witnessed FGM. But that was the moment I lost a little faith in the life I had always known. I went back to playing, helping my mother, school, but there was doubt, and there was fear.

It was several years later, when I was seven years old, that my family life truly began falling apart.

In Maasai culture, boys start herding the smaller animals—the sheep and goats—when they are little, often as young as four. They carry big sticks, often bigger than they are, and wander through the grazing lands all day. At night, they bring the animals into their pens, and the fathers come out and count their animals. It is a big responsibility for such small boys, but it is part of the cycle of life for our men: first herding sheep and goats, and then moving on to taking care of cows, becoming a warrior, marrying, raising a family, and counting your own cattle when you are old.

Before he reached school age, my younger brother started herding alongside the other boys. He was proud of his job, and my parents were proud of him. I missed my little playmate when he was out with the animals. No more mud chapatis for us. I was home with my mother and Soila. Women's work was much less exciting than playing. But I was proud, and a bit jealous, of my little brother.

The boys regularly crossed streams. Most of the time, there was little danger. Our part of Kenya was fairly arid, and the streams were tame.

One day there had been heavy rains. The streams moved fast, carrying pieces of wood and stones that had washed from the banks. My little brother was not afraid. The boys needed to cross, so they plunged in.

He didn't make it. His feet slipped out from under him, and the waters hurled him downstream, his body thrown against a rock like one more piece of storm debris.

The other boys could not reach him. They were not much bigger than my brother. It was Sunday morning, and I was at church with most of the adults. The boys ran screaming, and the people in the church ran toward the river. I followed, hoping the boy they were screaming about was not my brother.

By the time we reached the water, his body was limp.

I kept waiting for him to open his eyes. He looked the same as always. At any moment, he would cough out the water and start breathing. He just needed someone to hold him and warm him.

Why weren't the adults fixing this? Why were they letting him lie there? Why didn't they do something?

Some adults rushed Soila and me away. I did not want to leave my brother. I turned my head, trying to see him, even as they pushed me away. I wanted to shake him.

He will get better, I thought. *The adults will take care of him, and he will start breathing again. He cannot possibly be gone. He will come to, laughing at our sad faces.*

But he didn't. I never saw my brother again.

Life went on, but the ache did not go away. My father still managed the group ranches. He improved the game preserve and earned honors for his efforts.

My mother still took care of the family. Still brought tea to my father's guests. Soila and I still went to school.

Every evening, though, I would look up when the other boys came home with the cattle. Every evening, I felt fresh hurt when my brother was not with them.

We all felt hollow, as if the loss had carved us out and left us empty. Everything felt stiller, quieter. Little things would remind me of him. I could not eat chapatis. I no longer laughed and joked when I went to gather firewood. Without him as my partner to play games, I had no interest in them at all.

I missed my brother, but I also missed the family we once had. I would hear my mother start the first few notes of the songs that Maasai mothers sing about their sons, and then silence would fall. My father smiled less and sometimes told me to go away while he was working. My elder brother found reasons to be away working. I stayed by Soila's side, and she did not even complain about what a terrible housekeeper I was. At night she let me creep closer to her in bed and snuggle against her, and the two of us would cry together.

Wasting

The game preserve was successful enough that people far from Kenya noticed. A UK charity named it the best community conservancy and flew my father to London to receive the award. I tried to imagine flying in an airplane and visiting exotic places like England. I was proud of having such a great man as a father. I remember hoping that someday I could do my part to bring progress to our community.

We missed him while he was gone. Maasai men are often away from home for several nights, following the cattle as they graze, but we always knew they were nearby, on familiar lands. My father had gone someplace I could not even imagine. When he returned home, dusty and wrinkled, I would not stop hugging him.

"Let your poor father rest, Nice," my mother would finally say.

My father would laugh. "It is good to be home."

A few months after my brother's death, my father started losing weight. Of course he did. Who wants to eat when he has lost his son? But he kept getting thinner, and he started to slow down. His smile was smaller.

My mother cooked his favorite meals. She combed his hair and sang to him. Nothing worked. He grew thinner and moved more slowly.

"Something is wrong," his best friend said. "You need to go to the hospital in Nairobi."

My father was gone for a week. The house was even emptier. Without my father to follow, I never left Soila's side.

"Did you clean the cups from breakfast?" Soila asked.

"I will soon," I said.

"You always wait for tomorrow," she said. "And tomorrow never comes."

That was silly. Tomorrow always comes, clean cups or not. But I did what she asked. Staying close to Soila, with her watchful eyes, meant more work for me, but at least I was not lonely.

"Where has Nice gone? Seems like she is never around," she would say gently when she caught me daydreaming. She never raised her voice.

We did not talk about our lost brother. If we did, we would start crying. Instead, we told each other stories. Since neither of us could remember exactly how my grandmother would tell them, we would make up our own versions. Soila's were always sensible. Mine would go off in all directions: the trickster rabbit would go to Nairobi and come back with a bag of jawbreakers, or he would sneak onto a plane to London and meet the queen. Soila would shake her head at my stories, but she would also laugh and ask for more.

She sang to me and rubbed my back at night. It was like having a second mother.

I did not realize how deep her grief was at the time. When I was a toddler running off and playing, Soila had been by my mother's side, helping with my little brother. In a way, she had lost a son and a brother too. I think caring for me helped fill a bit of that empty spot he left inside her.

I had faith that things would change for the better, that a piece of our old life would come back. *When Father gets back,* I thought, *he will be healthy. It will be like before.*

But when he returned, he was even thinner. He slept late and went to bed early. He did not walk or bike to see his constituents; he hardly left the house at all. I would not leave his side, so my mother dragged my mattress into his room. I held his hand and sang as he went to sleep. *If I hold on tight enough,* I thought, *he will stay with us. We can make him better.*

When I asked about his illness, no one seemed to know what was wrong.

"Someone is jealous of him," one person would say. "It is poison."

"He ate some bad food when he went off to London," another would say.

No one could agree on what caused his pain, and no one had a solution to make him better.

One day I was rubbing lotion on his skin, and I saw underneath his shirt. His once strong chest was sunken, and thick pink scars ran across his brown skin. *They did something horrible to him in Nairobi,* I thought. I closed my eyes, lowered his shirt, pretended I had not seen.

He grew weaker, but I knew he still cared about me. He asked about school, and he made sure I did not skip my homework in order to sit with him. He would ask for a favorite song and tell Soila and me to be good girls and help our mother.

Within weeks, he could not get out of bed. He slept most of the day. His handsome face was hollow and bony. He stopped asking questions and drifted more and more into his own world.

There was nothing we could do. *Get better,* I prayed. *Come back to us.*

Soon he was sleeping nearly all the time. His age-mates had to lift him to use the restroom. He muttered to people long dead and did not seem to see the living. I would hold his hand harder when he drifted, hoping he would come back.

The game scouts received fancy new uniforms for the game ranch. The boys my father had employed instead of punishing for killing lions wanted to show him their uniforms. He could not get out of bed, so they came to him. We dragged his mattress outside and over to the side of the house, and he sat and watched them march in front of him. Those boys he had worked so hard training looked clean, crisp, and official. As weak as he was, he managed to smile.

He spoke to the boys: "I am proud of you. We have built this park, not the West. Our children and grandchildren will reap the benefits. I see you before me, strong young men, warriors for our land and people, and I know I can rest easy. You are the future of Kenya. You are the future of the Maasai."

For a moment, he was back, and I saw that old strength in his face. I had hope. His tongue was not heavy at all. *Maybe he is coming back to us,* I thought. *Maybe things are finally turning.*

As soon as the boys left, though, he drifted away once more. The game scouts' parade was the last time I saw him awake and fully aware of his surroundings. He slept on and off, eyes not really seeing even when they were open. I held his hand each night, and one day, as I slept, someone softly pulled my hand from his. I found out later that they carried him to a waiting car. When I woke up, I was alone, and his bed was cold. I did not get to say goodbye.

Another Loss

I was only seven when my father died. I did not understand why they took him away from me, why I could not go with him to the hospital. Looking back, I realize that at the time, my father had seven living children. We could not have stayed with him in the hospital, and my family did not have enough money for us to stay in a hotel in Nairobi. Even if we could have managed the trip, seven active children would not have made the last hours of a weak, tired, suffering man more comfortable.

I also did not think of how my mother must have felt. Her husband and life partner was suffering far away, and she must have realized he was not coming back. She took care of us and did her work the same as always, but her thoughts must have constantly been with him.

I also did not realize that, like my father, she was ill. She must have known that every pain and indignity my father suffered was waiting for her as well.

My mother had started losing weight while my father was sick. She was busy with the children and caring for him, and people assumed she was not taking the time to eat. But even after he died, she kept growing thinner.

"Are you feeling okay, Mother? Do you want to rest?" Soila asked one day as they did laundry together. Mother walked slowly and sometimes had coughing fits if she moved too quickly.

"We need to finish hanging these clothes," was all my mother said in response. They tossed the wet laundry over bushes so that it would dry in the sun and smell like fresh warm air.

My mother milked the cows, went for water, cooked for us. I saw how tired she was at night, so even I did my share of chores. The work was good for me. When I was busy, I did not remember my brother, did not cry for my father, did not worry about my mother.

I was only seven, though, and still apt to run in front of her when she was carrying water or hot soup.

"Go gather wood," she would say, sighing, even if we already had enough.

Soila was quieter and steadier. "Listen to your mother," she would say. "I'll help here."

It was easier outside, where I would look for wood or walk for water. Doing the normal things let me be in my body for a while. Being away from my mother let me forget how tired she had grown, how small her voice sounded. Sometimes I stopped and played with the other children, and I was a child again for a while.

My mother's clothes were loose. Her hair started coming out in clumps. She had always taken time to put her shining black hair in beautiful braids. Now it was as thin as an old woman's.

One morning, my mother could not get out of bed. Clumps of hair lay on her pillow.

"Soila," she whispered, "get some water and a razor."

"Your hair..." I said.

"I am not vain, child. It is too much trouble. Soila, go."

Soila gently lathered my mother's head. No one talked, and the quiet sounds of her hands at work seemed impossibly loud in that little room. I can still hear the sound of the razor scraping against my mother's head.

When Soila was done, my mother looked shrunken, a stranger to me.

My mother tried to laugh. "It is better this way, children. One less thing to care for."

As Soila carried off the dirty water so she could clean the bowl, she said nothing, but I noticed she was crying. I followed her out, grasping for her skirt. She put the bowl down, turned around, and grabbed me tightly in her arms.

"It is just hair," she whispered, but she cried just as hard as I did.

A few days later, my mother sent Soila and me to live across the river with our aunty Grace, her sister. I did not understand why we were going. I wanted to be with my mother.

"It is just a break, to give her time to rest," the adults said.

I knew better. Soila knew better. We had seen what had happened to our father. We knew our mother was just as ill.

I was in bed, half asleep, when my aunt called for Soila. I heard her wail, and I knew. I could not breathe. My stomach was tight. I closed my eyes, pretending to sleep. *It cannot be true,* I thought. *Make it not be true.*

I felt empty and raw from all the tears, and most of all, I felt utterly alone.

Later that night, as we lay in bed together, I begged Soila not to leave me too. "Promise," I said. "You have to promise."

She pressed into my back and put her arms around me. "No matter what," she said, "I will always be your family."

Both of my parents died without me. For years, I was not sure if they died in the hospital or at someone's home. What had killed them? Were they alone and scared? Were they in pain? Did they want to see their children one last time?

My family wanted to protect Soila and me by not having us watch our parents die. They thought we were too young to understand any details about their disease or treatment. I understand that now. At the time, though, it felt as if my parents had disappeared. It felt as if we had been abandoned. And not knowing what they actually suffered, the pain I envisioned was far worse than it might have truly been.

Only recently have I begun to ask my family what happened. I found out that my father died at the hospital, his best friend by his side. My mother's father took her to the hospital, and she died surrounded by family. Both were loved and cared for. Learning that was a relief. I could put to rest the worst of my fears. I could not be with them, but at the end they were with people they loved.

At the time, all I knew was that my father went to Nairobi and never came back. My mother sent me away, and I never saw her again. The safe, happy world I knew was gone. For Soila and me, childhood was over.

But we were not grown-ups. We still had one ritual left: the cut.

My Father's Legacy

My father always told me that the most important thing for our family and the Maasai was getting an education. He wanted to make sure that Soila and I, as well as my other brothers and sisters, finished school. Not just for ourselves but to improve the entire community.

Shortly before he died, he held a *harambee*. *Harambee* is a Swahili word meaning "all work together." Everyone comes and contributes what they can.

My father could have been a rich man, but he gave money away throughout his life, and the people in the group ranches knew it. They wanted to help the man who had given so much to them, so they came together and raised money for his family.

I remember walking around the gathering, listening to the adults talking about how much work he had done for the community. A woman remembered him helping her son buy a school uniform. A man remembered my father helping him get medicine for his wife. Everyone seemed to be telling one another these stories. I walked around proudly listening to all the people who thought my father was a great man. I did not understand that their stories all seemed to be in the past tense. I did not understand that the *harambee* meant that my father would soon be gone.

After he died, there was plenty of money to send us to school and give us a start in life, and there was land for us to make a home. Years later, I was told that the community had raised over one and a half million Kenyan shillings, the equivalent of more than fourteen thousand U.S. dollars. In rural Kenya, it was a fortune.

But Soila and I were young when our parents died. We were primary school girls who knew nothing about money. We depended on the kindness of others. My uncle, one of my father's brothers, controlled the *harambee* money.

My mother had made a will; she wanted her children to live together with Aunty Grace. After my mother died, the men in the family ignored her wishes. After all, my mother was a woman, and her sister was not part of the family. In Maasai culture, when a woman marries, she joins her husband's family and his age-set; her ties from childhood are severed. My mother's sister did not have any official role in our lives.

Instead, we went to live with my father's family members. For a short while—too short—my elder brother, Soila, and I all went to live together with the man I call my grandfather. In Maasai culture, any man who takes responsibility for a person is a "father." When my father was young, about eight or nine, he moved in with his brother. I am not sure exactly why, though I suspect it was because my grandparents had trouble supporting their children financially. So even though my "grandfather" was my father's brother, we called him Grandfather.

One morning, only a few months after my mother's death, my uncle came to my grandfather's house while my grandfather was with his cattle. He did not smile or even greet the children.

"Soila and you," he said, pointing at my elder brother "you are coming to live with me. Get your things."

"No!" I yelled.

My uncle stared at me, saying nothing. Soila ran to hug me. My brother spat on the ground and then turned back toward the house.

"I said get your things," my uncle said. Soila nodded, let me go, and began tying up her few clothes in her *losa*. My brother said nothing.

"Don't take them, please," I said. "I will work harder. I will be good. Please."

My uncle stared down at me. "Do not talk back to your elders, child. It has been decided."

I felt so tiny. I knew he was right. What could I do? I watched them walk away until the dust behind them settled. "They are all I have," I said, but there was no one left to hear. My voice sounded strange and loud in my head.

At my uncle's house, Soila worked like an adult, though she was only ten. We saw each other when we could, and it seemed as though every time I saw her, she was taller, more grown-up.

My brother stayed with another uncle. He was twelve and, at least in his own opinion, ready to take care of himself. He had a temper— he still does—and when my uncle gave him orders, he fought them. Almost every day, my uncle's small house was filled with screaming. Not long after he moved to my uncle's house, my brother dropped out of school, and soon after, he moved out. He could not afford his own home and he did not have cattle of his own, so he struggled to find a bed each night, but at least the fighting was over.

Soila and I could go to boarding school together, I thought, and be a family. I could help Soila with her writing, and she could help me with my math. We would live in the same dorm and be a family again. Our parents would look down on their girls and be proud of our learning.

I went to my uncle to ask for school fees from the *harambee* money. "There is no money," he said.

Maasai children are taught not to question their elders. Even with all I had been through, I wanted to be a good girl. I said meekly, "All I need is tuition."

"You are fine," my uncle said. "You will go to the local school." Soila and I had already learned all we could at the local level, and we needed a more rigorous school if we were going to continue our education.

As rudimentary as my education would be, at least I still went to school. Like my elder brother, my half brothers and sisters soon dropped out. Before my father died, he asked my uncle to take care of them. "Make sure they go to school," he told his brother. His first wife, he worried, might not take care of them, and unlike my mother and father, she did not value education. When my father died, the children were divided among family members. Though my father's brother honored his wishes in taking in the children, he did not make sure they went to school. Instead, he asked them to work cleaning his house, herding his animals, tending his farm. My half brothers and sisters did not have time for both that work and school, and no one urged them to continue their studies. One by one, they dropped out.

If they had owned land, my elder brother and the others might have tried farming and saved enough to buy their first goats and cows. Like the money, though, the lands had disappeared. When they went to stay with the rest of the family, the uncles told my brothers and sisters that their care was expensive. "Sign over the land," the uncles said, "and we will take care of it. We will pay you to use it."

But the money never materialized, and there was never talk of giving the land back. My brothers and sisters had to work on other people's farms for a few dollars a day. They helped pour concrete for other people's homes. They were the poorest of the Maasai, people without cattle. They had nothing but one another.

It took only a few months to unravel my father's legacy. All those years of working for the betterment of his children, all those years of encouraging us to go to school, and so quickly it was gone. Later I wondered why the rest of the family did not confront my uncle, did not ask where the money was or pitch in when what we had was gone. Some must have assumed he used the *harambee* money to take care of us; after all, he took in Soila, one of my father's children. Some must have assumed he did what he thought was best, invested the money in land and animals that helped the family to prosper. Maybe they thought it was not important to send children to school; my father's views on education were not shared by everyone. I am not sure what they were thinking, but they abandoned us. If my parents' children were going to get an education, it would be something we did on our own.

Home with Grandfather

Unlike my brothers and sisters, I had one adult looking after my interests. My grandfather loved my father, and he cared for me.

He used to call me *twiga,* meaning "giraffe" in Swahili, because I was tall. "We need to feed this *twiga,*" he would say when he came home at the end of the day. "Look how skinny she is." He would pat me on the head and smile.

That Christmas, he bought me clothes and handed them to me. "Try not to get any taller, little *twiga,*" he said, "or you will not have anything to wear. You are outgrowing these faster than the cotton plants can grow."

He also handed me a small bag of hard candies because, he said, I had been such a sweet girl. I was grateful for his gifts, and for his kindness in giving them, but I frowned when I thought of Soila and the others. I knew that my brothers and sisters did not have anyone buying them Christmas gifts.

My grandfather was a devout Christian. Each evening, he would lead us in prayer and tell us stories from the Bible, and even now that he is older, he never misses church on Sunday. Much of what I know of God I know from his teaching.

I was lucky in that he honored my father's wishes for my education. He was not a wealthy man, and the money from the *harambee* never made it into his hands, so there was not enough to pay for boarding school fees. There was a local school, though, and I was grateful for that. Every evening when my grandfather was home, he asked me if I had obeyed my teacher that day and if I had done my schoolwork.

Like my father, he worked in politics to improve the lives of the Maasai. A few years before I was born, with my father's support, he had served as a member of parliament. That office did not mean that he was wealthy—he was from a poor, rural district—but it did mean that he was respected. People would stop and talk when he walked by, just as they had with my father. My father campaigned for his older brother.

But despite the respect he had earned for his years of service, my grandfather realized that, without my father's support, he would not have a political career. At my father's funeral, he said, "My career dies along with him." He understood that his brother and honorary son had given him much of the little he had.

My grandfather's wife was kind, and she watched out for me as if I were her own. Her children had moved into their own homes, so I had her to myself. She disciplined me when I did not do my work or showed disrespect, but she praised my schoolwork, made sure I ate, and combed my hair.

She suffered from diabetes and high blood pressure, and she was often sick in bed. But she cooked for my grandfather every day, and she kept her home spotless. In the afternoon, we would walk to the small plot where she grew tomatoes and onions, and I would help her carry the vegetables back home. She showed me how to slice the vegetables and add them to the pan. She showed me how to cook my grandfather's favorite dishes the way he liked.

She had to take insulin. Because my grandfather's wife could not ask a man to assist her with such a personal matter, one of us would hold her clothes while the other prepared the needle and injected her leg or abdomen. "I am glad you are here, Nice," she said when I helped. "I cannot have a man see me being immodest, and you are a good helper."

She was not a replacement for my parents—nothing could have been—but she helped make an unbearable time bearable.

About a year after I came to live with my grandfather, though, she had to go to the hospital, and like my father, she never came back. I would have been only about eight when she died. After so many deaths, her loss left me empty. I am sure I cried and grieved, but what I remember most is hollowness. As if I had been wrung dry. Most of all, as if I was tiny and alone.

Alone

A few months after his wife's death, my grandfather married again. My grandfather's new wife did not share his affection for me. Gone were my days of escaping to read a book when I was supposed to be doing the dishes. I was still only eight, but I had to be the first one out of bed in the morning to make tea. When she gave birth the following year, it became my job to feed her new baby. I had to wash the diapers and hang them out to dry. I had to make sure the men of the house—my grandfather, uncles, and cousins, even a few farmhands—were fed. The baby had to be dressed and ready before I was allowed to walk the six miles to school. Many mornings, I would be late, and I would get hit on the backside and shamed in front of my classmates.

On the way back from school, I gathered fuel for the fire. I would carry it, wrapped in a cloth, on my back. At home, I had to clean the dirty clothes and hang them to dry, sweep out the house, and make dinner. I would not eat until the rest of the family had eaten—if anything was left, that is. Since the men and women ate separately, my grandfather did not know that his wife wasn't feeding me. I was often hungry. Sometimes my aunty Grace would stop by with good food, even fresh bananas, but my grandfather's wife would take the food for herself and her own family.

There was no time to study. Sometimes, tired from the constant work, I fell asleep at my desk at school, and I earned a swat on the hand or the buttocks. I worked hard enough to get passing marks, but it felt as though there was never enough time for school. I certainly did not learn all that I might have.

Nothing I did was right. A badly cooked meal meant a beating. A dirty spot on a blanket meant a beating. A frown or a tear meant I was beaten even harder.

When she was particularly angry with me, my grandfather's wife locked me in the kitchen, a small structure separated from the main house, overnight. I had never slept in a building alone before, and I could hear animals howling through the thin walls. The dirt floor was cold and hard against my bruises. I could feel mice skittering across my hands or feet while I slept. When I woke in the morning, I was so stiff and sore it was hard to move, so I would do a poor job at my chores and earn another beating.

When my grandfather was home, I slept in a bed like everyone else. I ate the same food as the rest of the family. I never got beaten. Like other Maasai men, though, he was often gone, tending to his cattle and taking care of his business, so mostly I was a free maid for his wife.

I ran away. More than once. I would run on foot, or sneak onto a bus and hope no one tried to collect my fare. Sometimes I ran to Soila. She would find a friend who'd let me sleep on her floor, but Soila had nowhere to hide me at my uncle's home. She saw that I was skinny and sneaked me a little food. She did not have much more than I did, so my eating meant that she went without. If my uncle caught her sheltering me, Soila would get a beating.

More often, I fled to my aunty Grace's house. She would always feed me and make sure I had a bath. For a night or two, I had a home where I was safe and loved.

The first time I ran to her house, Aunty Grace asked me why I was there. "You have always been so good, Nice. What is wrong at home?"

"Nothing," I said.

"Nothing makes you take a bus and run to my house? Nothing makes you dishonor your grandfather?"

"I miss home," I said.

She was quiet for a moment. "Are you sure that is all, Nice?" she said.

I nodded. I had been brought up to always obey adults and show them respect. Telling on my grandfather's wife felt like insulting my grandfather.

The next time I ran to her, Aunty Grace asked me the same questions, and I answered the same way. The next time, she stopped asking. I never spoke against my grandfather's wife, but looking back, I realize that Aunty Grace must have suspected that I was being mistreated. As part of my mother's family, and a woman at that, she had no way to stop the abuse. All she could do was welcome me in and give me what love she could before someone came to drag me away.

My grandfather's wife told him that I was lazy and disobedient, that I flirted with all the men in the neighborhood, so my grandfather began to suspect I was running off to see a boyfriend. Those suspicions hurt almost as much as the beatings. He thought I was lying, that I had failed him. Even so, I could not tell him that his wife was cruel to me. I told him I missed my old family, which was true, but I did not tell him the entire truth. He had loved my father, and he loved me, and I did not want to make him suffer.

Worse was the fear that, if I told him, he would blame me. If his wife punished me, it must be because I deserved it. I started to think she was right, that I did deserve it. She was not cruel to her own child. There must be a reason I was treated differently. I must be a bad child. I was the kind of girl who ran from my problems. My cheeks did not have the round ritual scars of other Maasai girls because I had run away when they tried to burn me. I had proven I was a coward again by running to my aunt's house. I was not strong. I was not worthy.

Now that I am an adult, I know more about child abuse. I know that children hide what is happening behind closed doors because of shame and fear. I wish there was some way the adult me could reach back and offer some comfort and hope to that grieving little girl.

I got some relief when another Soila, my cousin, came to live with us. With her beside me, there was someone to share the work. We talked while we cooked and cleaned, quietly so we did not annoy my grandfather's wife, and that alone made the work a little easier. When we gathered wood, out of earshot of the house, we would laugh together, just like normal children. Being with someone who did not hate me made me realize that, maybe, I did not deserve to be hated. Even locked in the kitchen at night, I did not feel as cold on that dirt floor with a warm body beside me.

On Sundays we were not allowed to go to church with the family. We were expected to stay home and have a meal ready when they returned. I missed church. But in some ways Sunday was the best time of the week. Soila and I could make ourselves pancakes and eggs, and for once we could eat until we were full. We talked as loudly as we wanted and laughed together.

Those moments of laughter did not come often, though. Most of the time, I said nothing. I did my work. I cried silently, and only when I was alone. If no one saw me, no one hit me. I was already small. I did everything I could to shrink to nothing.

The Last Beating

One day I wore a pair of pants. I am not sure where I got them. My school uniform was a simple dress with a collar. I did not have any money to buy myself clothes. Maybe someone at school gave me a hand-me-down.

When my grandfather's wife saw the pants, she stopped cold. Maasai women did not wear pants. "Take those off," she said. "You look like a prostitute."

I nodded my head and headed to the other room.

"No," she said, "take them off right now. Take everything off."

I looked around the room. Her cousins, all men, were sitting there. I did not move. At eight, almost nine, I was just starting to develop the hints of the curves of a woman's body, and I did not want the men to see me.

She started beating me with a stick, but it was better than being naked in front of the men. She beat me until I collapsed on the floor.

When I was strong enough to stand up, she told me to take off my clothes or she would beat me again. Slowly, I took off my clothes and stood shivering. I could not look up, could not see the eyes of the people around me. I was ashamed.

She hit me again.

"You are going to end up just like your parents!" she screamed. "You are going to die of AIDS!"

I could not breathe, could not even feel the pain of her punches anymore. It was her words that hurt most. *No,* I thought, *it is not true, it cannot be.*

When she was finished, she sent me to the kitchen, where I started crying. I hated her for saying that about my parents.

I hated her for being right.

I thought about what had happened to my parents. The strange illness when they were still young. The way their bodies wasted away. The fact that a husband and a wife died so close together.

People were dying of AIDS throughout sub-Saharan Africa. It was a virus, not a moral failing. At the time, though, people viewed it as something shameful, a disease of prostitutes and immoral city people. People who died of AIDS brought shame to their families.

I did not know what caused AIDS. I did not even know why people thought it was a scandalous disease. I knew it was whispered about. I knew it meant my parents were bad. All I really understood was that my parents were gone, and that people were so ashamed of the reason that they would not even discuss what had killed them.

I felt foolish for not figuring it out before. I was embarrassed to have listened to the lies people told me. How could my father possibly waste away eating bad food in London? It made no sense.

My cousin Soila came and held me that night. I cried and nestled by her side. I did not tell her about my parents. To her, it must have seemed that I was crying from the beating.

"All we have to do is get through this day," she said, "and someday this will be over."

She stroked my hair and let me sob. I quieted finally. Though I was still hiccuping, my nose running and my face swollen, I felt better. I still felt confused. I still hurt at the insult to my parents. It still hurts today. But Soila was right. I just had to get through each day.

I decided that my grandfather's wife could not take my parents' memories from me. I knew my parents. I knew how much they had loved their families. How much they had loved their people. They had lived for others; they were good. I knew that my mother had been a godly woman and my father a good husband. It did not matter what had killed them.

I was going to prove my grandfather's wife wrong. I was not going to be a prostitute. I was not going to be a disgrace. I was going to be someone.

Fighting to Learn

I went to my grandfather the next day and asked to go to boarding school. My dream of going away with Soila was dead, but I might still escape.

Going to school was not just about escape, though. It was about my parents' dream. I had heard my grandfather's wife insult my parents for dying of AIDS. But their lives had been much more than how they died. Their greatest dream was education. I was a little girl. I did not have much power. But I knew I could learn.

"Don't you want to stay with us?" my grandfather said.

I did not want to lie to him, but I did not want to hurt him either. "You have been good to me, but I want to learn."

He nodded. It would be a financial struggle. But he knew how much I was grieving and how much school had meant to my parents.

"We will try to find a way," he said.

"I will move closer to town so I can work," I said. I was glad for the excuse. The truth was, after that last beating, after the insult to my parents, I had vowed never to spend another night under that roof.

I dug up the small stash of coins I had saved and hidden in a hole in the kitchen. I hugged my cousin Soila goodbye. I did not bother to tell my grandfather's wife that I was going.

My half brothers and half sisters lived in a small house together, and even though it was crowded, they made room for me. It was not much, but it was better than nursing my bruises on the kitchen floor.

I went to the uncle who had managed the *harambee* money. I bent my head to show him respect, but he did not touch my head in return. I do not know what I had done to offend him—maybe it was the shame he felt for having taken so much from his brother's children, maybe some resentment he had hidden from my father for years—but he was not willing to make that small gesture to accept me.

"What do you want?" he asked.

I asked for my school fees. If he could not spare the money outright, could he make a loan? When I got a job, I could repay him.

"Come back tomorrow," he said.

When I returned the next day, one of my cousins said that he was out.

I came back again the following day, and the day after that. He was never home.

One day I saw him standing with some other men in the fields. I started to walk toward them, and he turned his back on me. I realized that I would never see any of the money my father had set aside for us.

I was determined to find a way.

Maasai women typically undergo FGM and marry around the time they begin menstruating. Their days start before dawn with cooking, gathering firewood, doing laundry, caring for children, and hauling water. (Giulio Paletta)

My work allows me to see the faces of the young girls for whom the future means education and progress. (Jeroen van Loon)

When we fight FGM as a community, including each generation, we have the most success. (Giulio Paletta)

Many strong Maasai women stand by my side in the fight against FGM. (Humberto Tan)

On important occasions, I wear traditional Maasai beads sewn together by Aunty Grace. Fighting for girls does not mean giving up the beautiful aspects of our culture. (Jeroen van Loon)

In this photo I was appearing before King Felipe of Spain. (Fundación Princesa de Asturias)

Traditionally, Maasai women had no public voice. Through a lot of hard work and persistence, I was able to earn the right to speak. Someday, all girls will have the same right. (Giulio Paletta)

My sister, Soila. She is my rock of courage, and we have managed to build a life together. (Jeroen van Loon)

We celebrated the groundbreaking for A Nice Place with an Alternative Rites of Passage ceremony. Our donors witnessed firsthand the difference we can make in the lives of these girls. (Joost Bastmeijer)

My grandfather was the first man I had to convince to allow me freedom and education. I'm proud to have him stand by my side at the groundbreaking for A Nice Place as we move forward with our work. (Joost Bastmeijer)

Aunty Grace has supported me throughout my life, as she supported my parents. Here my mother (left) and Aunty Grace campaign for my father. (Author's personal collection)

I look forward to the day when Maasai girls can honor their heritage while also honoring themselves. (Luca Antonio Marino)

The nearest boarding school was not terribly expensive. Most of the students there are from poor, rural Kenyan towns. But to me, the amount of money seemed immense.

The local farms, the ones my mother had helped pioneer, would hire workers to lend a hand for a few shillings a day. I worked there. Once I was at boarding school, I could take in laundry. I could run errands for teachers and other students. Whatever I needed to do, I would do it.

Aunty Grace made beautiful beadwork; the Maasai were famous for their intricately beaded necklaces. She sold them to tourists and gave some of the money to me.

My sister, Soila, worked on the farms by my side. She gave her share of the money to me. I felt bad taking it from her—her life at my uncle's house was not that different than mine had been at my grandfather's—but she wanted me to have it. She wanted at least one of us to live the dream of our parents.

"Besides," she said, "if Uncle found out about the money, he would take it as payment for the food I eat."

With all of us working together, we managed to raise enough—barely—for me to start boarding school.

I felt bad leaving the other Soila, my cousin, alone with my grandfather's wife, but fortunately, she moved on soon after I left. Of all the children in my family, the two of us, the ones who had to work for everyone else, who often did not have enough food, who were beaten...we were the only ones who managed to finish high school.

New Beginning

My boarding school was about an hour away from Kimana by car, many hours by foot.

The first time I walked there, my grandfather came with me. The school required its students to bring a foam mattress, sheets, and a towel, and he carried my supplies for me. I carried a small bundle containing my clothes, a few pencils, and a bar of soap.

The buildings were simple: concrete blocks and stucco, metal roofs, dusty grounds. The school was clean and well kept, but it was hardly a place of ivy-covered halls and oak-paneled classrooms. But when I saw those simple structures, I smiled and stood a little straighter. The bare-bones buildings looked grand to my eyes. I was going to learn. I was going to be a real student.

My grandfather left me at the gate. "Make us proud, Nice," he said.

I thought of his kindness in welcoming me into his home. I thought of his smile when he called me *twiga*. I did not think of his wife at all. I was going to make him proud, I swore to myself. I nodded and smiled but did not say anything back. I knew that if I tried to speak, I would end up crying.

*   *   *

Our dormitory was one large room crowded with metal bunks. I found an empty one and made my bed. A few girls had already arrived and were talking by their bunks. I smiled at them. Maybe I should have been nervous about whether I could keep up with the work. Maybe I should have worried about whether I would fit in. Instead, I felt free. I knew I was out of danger, surrounded by girls who would soon be my friends. Throughout the afternoon, more girls arrived, some tense and stiff, some smiling widely. By the end of the afternoon, most of us were laughing together.

At my boarding school, the students came from many miles away. Few Maasai girls were educated past elementary school—none, as far as I knew, from my town. So even though the school was in a predominantly Maasai area, most of the girls and teachers were non-Maasai. FGM is practiced in about thirty of over forty Kenyan ethnic groups. Many groups who practice it do so at lower rates than among the Maasai. So for Kenyan women, it is hardly a universal practice. For the first time in my life, I kept company with girls who would not get the cut.

Some girls were curious, asking the Maasai girls who had been through the cut but were not yet married to show them their scars. They pulled at our towels in the showers, wanting to compare us. I held on to my towel extra tightly and tried to avoid those girls.

Even that teasing had a good side. It showed me that there was another way, that getting the cut was not the natural thing I had always been taught it was. That maybe I could find a way not to get it and still find a place in the world.

Without the long walk to and from school, without the constant labor, I had time to study. I slept better in a bed and without bruises on my body. I stopped falling asleep at my desk. I still had to work hard, and I took in laundry and earned money in the fields, but the workload was never unreasonable. I became a good student, and my teachers noticed.

I had an English teacher, Miss Caroline, who was my favorite. She was a tall, slim, light-skinned woman with beautiful long hair. She always had a smile on her face, though she was not afraid to smack our hands if we misbehaved.

She was also Kamba, one of the larger ethnic groups in Kenya. Unlike the Maasai, the Kamba people do not practice FGM.

Miss Caroline told us that her door was always open, and since I did not have any adult women to talk to, I took her up on the offer. The first time I went to her office, I stood outside the open door. Would I be bothering her? Would I make her think less of me? I took a deep breath and, head down, walked slowly into the room.

"Is it okay to talk?" I asked.

"Always, Nice, always," she said, smiling.

The words came out in a rush. I talked about how much I missed my sister. How I missed my grandfather. Classes were challenging at my new school, much more challenging than the ones at the day school I had attended before, and I told her I was worried that I would never catch up. I was worried, I said, that I would not make my grandfather proud.

She nodded and listened, saying a word or two to encourage me, but mostly she sat quietly.

She did not even have to offer advice. When I was done speaking, my chest felt lighter. I think I might have smiled.

Then I froze. I realized that I had been talking for almost an hour. What had I done? Was she going to judge me? Was she going to think I was weak?

"Nice," she said, leaning toward me, "I am so glad we got to talk. I hope you come again."

I smiled. Of course I would.

"What would you like to do when you grow up, Nice?" she asked me one day.

That was the first time an adult had ever asked me that question. I did not have an answer.

The school was full of working women. Many, including Miss Caroline, did not have husbands. They seemed happy. Maybe, I thought, I could do something with my life.

I loved our English class. The language was infuriating—why do "caught" and "cot" look nothing alike and "tough" and "dough" look so similar?—but I could lose myself in the challenge.

After class, Miss Caroline handed me books. They were dog-eared, hand-me-down books for toddlers, but to me, they were precious. As I carefully sounded out the words (or got frustrated realizing that spelling often has no relationship to the sounds that make up the words), I was discovering a new world.

"You work hard," Miss Caroline said when I returned each book and asked for another. "Hard enough to continue your education. Think about it."

I did think. Could I finish boarding school? Could I go to college?

After class one day, she asked me to stay. "Nice," she said, "we need to talk."

She didn't have her usual wide smile. Had I done something wrong? Had I failed a test?

"I have taught Maasai girls before," she said.

I nodded.

"Not one has finished school. They go home. They get circumcised.

Maybe they come back for a month or two, but they always leave. I try to talk to them while they are still young. I let them know there is another way. Before they drop out and start having babies. Is that what you want, Nice?"

Of course not. I wanted to stay in school.

I was younger than most girls who got the cut. Usually, a Maasai woman watches her daughter. When she starts to grow tall, when her breasts start to bud, she knows it is time for the cut. The mother goes to the girl's father, and he arranges the ceremony.

The ceremony usually happens just before a girl enters puberty. The girls are still young, but they have weeks with their mothers, preparing for what is going to happen, gathering strength from her stories. As much as a person can prepare for something as terrible as female genital mutilation, the girls are ready.

No one had spoken to Soila and me about getting the cut, so I thought I had time. But eventually, it would happen.

"I have to get the cut," I said quietly.

"Does that mean dropping out of school? Think about it."

I knew that my parents had wanted me to get the cut, but I also knew they valued education. They would never want me to drop out of school. Did one thing make the other impossible, or was that an outdated tradition? I had never pieced it together, but maybe my teacher was right.

"Do you really have to get the cut?" she asked me.

Did I? Could I avoid the cut? The thought excited me, but it was frightening too. Shouldn't I want to marry and have children? Was there something wrong with me?

"I have time," I said. "The cut is years away."

"Whatever you decide," she said, "you can always come to me."

Running

I thought I had time. When I arrived home for my next school break, though, my uncle told Soila and me to walk with him to our grandfather's house. He rarely paid attention to us, so I knew something was happening. I grabbed Soila's hand and held it tightly.

"It is time for these girls to get the cut," my uncle said to my grandfather.

When I heard those words, I remembered the morning my mother had taken me to see the cut as clearly as if it had just happened. I pictured myself in the center of that semicircle, the women around me, holding me down. Choking back my screams until I was alone. Enduring the pain every woman in our community had suffered for hundreds of years.

I knew suddenly, clearly, that my teacher was right: as soon as the scars healed, my uncle would marry me off. I was still only eight, just about to turn nine. Not nearly old enough to get married. The man might be thirty or even older. There would be no more boarding school, certainly no college. The same would happen to Soila. We would not be able to watch out for each other; we would not even be considered a part of each other's families. One half sister had already been married off. The other had followed her boyfriend to another part of the country. We were the only sisters left.

This was it. This was the end of my parents' dreams and mine.

My belly ached at the thought of being with an old man. I knew men and women did something together in secret, something men liked and women did not. Would my husband expect that of me? Would there be a first wife who resented me? Would the man hit me? I would have to cook and clean and follow his orders. There would be no time for laughing and playing.

My grandfather hesitated. "Are you sure?" he said to my uncle. I was tall. As tall as many girls who get the cut at twelve or thirteen. But I was so young. When my grandfather looked at me, he saw a skinny little girl who still cried in the night over the death of her parents.

My uncle saw another mouth to feed. "We will need meat for the celebration," he said. "We have to pay the woman for the cutting. It is best to do all the girls at once."

He had three daughters. One ceremony for the five of us would be less expensive. And, as I found out much later, he saw profit in Soila and me. He was planning to claim our dowries.

My grandfather nodded. It was decided.

Two days later, at my uncle's house, our adult clothes were waiting for us. They were beautiful, a bright red top and blue skirt. No hand-me-downs. I loved the thought of dressing in a grown-up woman's clothing.

Then I saw the razor. My mouth grew dry when I looked at the sharp blade.

My cousins did not show any fear; they seemed excited. They were older than Soila and me, ready to become women. I also think they were ready to escape from my uncle's house. He beat them, and the beatings were worse than those I had endured from my grandfather's wife. Once, he beat one of his daughters so badly she coughed up blood. They wanted to escape that house, even if it meant the cut.

The only one I could talk to was Soila. My sister and I stayed up late into the night, whispering.

"I am afraid," I said. Soila would suffer the cut by my side, but that was not a comfort.

When our parents died, Soila held my hand and hugged me through the worst nights. She made sure I ate, kept my hair neat, and encouraged me to go to school. She was only a child herself, but she saved me. She was like my mother and my best friend. If she got the cut by my side, it only meant I was going to lose her.

"All girls get the cut, Nice," she said, but her voice was shaking as much as mine.

"I do not want to marry an old man," I said.

"Maybe he will be nice."

"He is going to touch you," I told her. "He might beat you. He is going to give you a baby."

"I will have a home."

"You will have to work all the time."

"I will have a family."

"We are a family."

"We do not have a choice."

"We can run."

My sister was silent for a long time. She was probably too old, I realize now, to believe in my childish fantasy of escape. But she could see how important this was to me, and she was terrified. Our mother had taken her to see a girl go through the cut too.

Maybe, Soila must have thought, *if we sisters stick together, there is a chance.*

So we ran from my uncle's house before dawn on the day of the ceremony. We climbed barefoot up a tree outside my uncle's house to hide. It was dark, the coldest part of the night, just before sunrise. I felt my sister shaking next to me, whether from cold or fear I cannot say. The leaves were thick, but not thick enough to hide two little girls once the sun rose.

We could hear the men laughing and singing, the softer voices of the women as they began to arrive at my uncle's house. The moon had set, so I could not see anyone, not even Soila next to me in the tree.

We knew if we fled along the roads, the men would chase us down on motorbikes. If we ran in the dark, we would not be able to see our way through the bush. Our town was isolated. We were surrounded by scrub, thorns, rocks, and wild animals, like lions. And hyenas. No Maasai left a village at night because of the hyenas. They could smell you from two miles away and track you for twenty miles, if necessary, until the pack saw its chance.

So we huddled in silence, waiting for sunrise.

After an hour, we saw our three cousins come to wash themselves with the water that had been left out overnight to chill, supposedly to numb the pain, as if a bit of cold water could blunt the agony of the cut. Then they walked back toward my uncle's house. Soila and I held ourselves rigid, moving nothing but our eyes.

Please, I begged silently, *do not look up.*

We could hear the men yelling for us, and we sunk down farther into ourselves. *Please,* I begged over and over, *please do not look up.*

When the light began to rise, we ran. It was fifteen kilometers through the bush to my aunt's house, and even when it started to get hot, even when the rocks and thorns cut our bare feet, we did not stop to rest.

My aunty Grace took us in. She picked the thorns from our feet and legs. In Swahili, the thorns are called "wait awhile" because if you do not relax and slowly pull them out, they will cut you badly. Soila and I could not afford to wait, not while we ran. Once we finally stopped moving, we were so torn up that we could not walk from the pain. After bathing, we slept most of the day. We were hurt, but we were safe and whole.

Two days later the men tracked us down. Of course they did. We were children, and our plans went no further than running away.

My aunt was our mother's sister; she loved us. But there was nothing she could do.

The men dragged us outside. "Shame!" they shouted. "Shame!" They called us names, told us we had embarrassed the family, beat us as we cried for them to stop.

My aunt had to watch, flinching with each hit.

I felt the sticks and fists, but worse, the humiliation. The men said I was a freak and a coward, and I felt like both. Women who did not get the cut were not part of the community. They would never marry or have children. They were not women at all.

Afterward, I cried. I ached. I felt utterly powerless. I watched Soila cry next to me, and I knew I was the cause.

But I was not defeated. I dried my tears and vowed I would not show my pain.

Hiding

I had escaped the cut, but I knew it was only temporary. I knew we could not run to my aunt again. My uncle had kept the men from beating her, but if she took us in again, nothing would stop them, and the community would turn against her as well.

Maybe I should just go ahead with it, I thought. In my community, the cut was universal; I had to get it sometime. If I agreed to go through with it, maybe my family would let me go back to school and finish my education.

After the break, I returned to boarding school. I told Miss Caroline that I had run. I asked her if I had done the right thing.

"Nice, have you thought about what we talked about before, about what you want to do with your life?"

"Maybe go to college," I said.

"If you get the cut," she said, "do you think that will happen?"

It would not. The cut does not take just a piece of a woman's body. It makes her eligible for marriage and for a lifetime of childbearing and servitude. It takes a woman's hopes and dreams. If I got the cut, marriage would follow.

I wanted my freedom. Being so close to losing my education made that clear.

But Maasai women tell girls that if they do not get the cut, they will never be real women. They will never get married or have children. They told me insects would grow inside my womb and eat me from the inside out. That my clitoris would keep growing until it was down past my knees.

Miss Caroline told me that those were just old wives' tales. "I didn't get the cut or get married," she said, "and do you see anything wrong with me? You've seen my children. I had them without getting the cut."

I still was not sure. She was not Maasai. Maybe the rules were different for us. I trusted Miss Caroline, but I was still very young, and what might seem silly to a grown-up was a real fear to a small girl.

"Look at the Bible, Nice. Does it say anything about the cut?"

"I do not know," I said. I had never heard a Bible story about the cut, but maybe it was in a part I had never seen.

"It does not. Not for girls. Wouldn't God have given us that rule if he wanted girls to get the cut?"

I knew she was telling the truth. The Bible did not mention the cut. And the world was not full of women with clitorises hanging down past their knees or wombs full of insects.

But knowing she was right and really believing it were different matters. I had been told the stories since I was a toddler. And my mother, my grandmother...every woman in my family for as far back as anyone could remember had had the cut. Who was I to break our tradition?

I wanted to belong.

I avoided going home. Generally, the Maasai perform the cut in April or December, during the rainy seasons. There is plenty of meat and milk for the celebration and to help the girls recover. And the weather is cooler. I stayed away during those times.

Sacrifice

But I could not avoid home forever, and as soon as I returned, my uncle announced that it was time. No running. No excuses. I had humiliated the family. He determined that I was not going to do it again.

There was less ceremony this time. My uncle's wife sat with Soila and me, telling us we had humiliated the family, that we were cowards, that we had to do our duty. There would be no new dresses this time, no lessons about becoming women. It was just Soila and me alone in a dark room, guarded by my aunt, waiting to become women in the morning. When she was finally convinced that we were asleep, she left us alone. I told Soila I was running again. I had been uncertain the first time I ran. Coming so close to the cut, to losing my education and my freedom, had chased that uncertainty away. I knew now that I would run a thousand times if I had to. I was not getting the cut. I was not getting married. I was going to school.

"Come with me," I said.

Soila was quiet. She had been living in our town, living with my uncle. There was no boarding school for her. If she did not get the cut, she would have to live with people constantly shaming her, telling her she was a coward.

"You go," she said at last.

She was the only family I had left.

I shook my head. "No," I said. "I need you."

"They will catch us. You know it."

I did know it. I remembered the last time.

I knew that this time they might be angry enough to hold me down and give me the cut then and there.

"If one of us gets the cut, maybe they will be happy," Soila said.

It was dark. I could see only the outline of her face.

"Let me do this for you, Nice," she said quietly.

She spoke with the voice of our mother. It was just like when we were smaller, and Soila protected me from bullies.

"You can go back to school, Nice. I am staying."

I knew she was right. I knew I could not change her mind. But that did not make it any easier to leave her.

It was close to dawn, and if I did not go then, I would never get away. I ran to the same tree and hid. Alone this time, I felt the cold more sharply, and I cried. I ached to go back to Soila, to be with her, but I knew I could not. As I waited there, I could hear the songs, and I knew that even if I went back it would be too late. She was already gone.

When it was light, I ran back to my school. It was much farther than my aunt's house, and no one was with me this time. When I finally arrived, it was late afternoon. My legs were shaking. I could barely breathe.

When Miss Caroline saw my bloody feet and the tears streaming down my dirt-stained face, she did not say anything. She understood what I was running from. She took me in, cleaned me, and gave me bandages. Then she hugged me and told me not to worry.

"Nice," she said, "you can stay with me. You are safe."

Speaking My Mind

My uncles came looking for me again at Miss Caroline's house. She kept her word and turned them away.

But I knew I could not hide forever. I knew my teacher would not always be there to protect me. I could run a thousand times, but if I did not convince my family to let me avoid the cut and stay in school, I would lose my freedom in the end. They could grab me, hold me down, and force the cut. I would never really be safe.

I had to get someone on my side.

On the next school break, I went to my grandfather. I bowed. He touched my head in return.

I sat before him, legs stretched in front of me in the posture that a polite young Maasai uses when speaking with an elder.

"Grandfather, I am sorry I ran," I said.

"Are you ready for the cut?"

I shook my head. "I mean, I am sorry I did not come to you. Not that I did not get the cut."

The words came out. I talked so fast, they tripped over my heavy tongue. I told him my dreams, how I wanted to go to school, how

I wanted to be the first in my family to go to college. I told him I was afraid of the cut. I told him I was afraid to get married. I told him I wanted to be like my father. I told him how I prayed to God every day to be reunited with Soila. How I wanted to save what was left of my family. How, if they tried to force me, I would run and keep running.

I had never spoken that way to an elder, and certainly not to a man. I was breathless when I was finished. I know I was not graceful or eloquent. Like my father, sometimes I have a heavy tongue. I was ashamed for talking so much, for being so disrespectful. But it felt good too, because I had been honest.

My grandfather was listening, but I was not sure my words would make an impact. I needed him to start thinking the way I did.

"What did my father want most for his children?" I asked.

"He wanted you educated," my grandfather said.

"Are all his children getting an education?" I asked.

He sighed. "It did not work out for most of you. I wish it had."

"If I do what Uncle wants, if I get the cut, will I get an education?"

"We will send you back to school," he said. "That I promise."

"Thank you, Grandfather. But how many girls finish school after the cut?"

He was silent for a while. He knew that girls never graduated. "I will let you finish," he said at last.

"Grandfather," I said quietly, "I am afraid."

He looked at me and sighed. "You are still very young."

"Yes," I said, nodding. "I need time."

"I will give you six months," he said. "Go back to school. They will not bother you."

My grandfather was the elder. The rest of my family could scowl at me. They could call me names. They could make me feel unwelcome. But he was the man in charge. With his support, they could not touch me.

I went to see Soila at my uncle's house. After a girl gets the cut, she spends weeks recovering. There are no painkillers or antibiotics. There is scabbing, bleeding, and a lot of pain and soreness. She gets fresh milk, blood, and meat to help her body heal. A lot of girls even get a little chubby. Soila had gone through all that alone. I had not been by her side to bear it with her. By the time I came home for school break, she was walking and doing her regular work.

We have never talked about what she experienced when she went through the cut. When I left her the morning of the ceremony, we both knew what was waiting for her. We did not have to speak of her suffering. We knew.

"I am so sorry, Soila," I said. "I should have made you come with me."

"No," she said. "There was no need. This is what I wanted."

I found out later that she did not flinch. There was not a large celebration the second time; we had brought shame to the family. But when Soila got the cut, she showed them her courage.

I still felt guilty, though, at the thought of her bleeding and hurting without me.

She came through it as well as could be expected. She did not lose too much blood. She did not get an infection or severe complications. Her health was not ruined, but she would never know sexual pleasure. She would always have to worry about health risks in the future.

And she was officially a Maasai woman, with all the limitations that entails.

*   *   *

At the end of six months, I visited my grandfather again and asked for six more. I was only nine, still young to get the cut. He agreed again to a postponement.

I could not visit Soila this time. She had been married and sent to another village. She had no choice in her spouse, or even whether to have a spouse at all. She did not control where or how the family would live. She had to build a new life with strangers.

I imagined her alone, frightened. I had not been there when she left with her husband; there had been no ceremony (though my uncle got a dowry for her). It might sound strange, but I am glad there was no wedding. A Maasai wedding is a time for tears. The ceremony would have been a sad one, and Soila and I had been through enough goodbyes.

As a young girl, she was taking on all the duties of an adult woman. And she would have to do it without any friendly faces to help her. People praise my courage in running away, but Soila was the one who showed real courage. She must have been scared. She must have felt lost and alone. But she did what was necessary to survive.

Aside from my grandfather, no one in town would speak to me. I stayed with my half brothers and sisters, but their eyes looked past me. They did not offer to share their food and would not eat what I made. I was shameful. The other children ran when they saw me coming. The adult women whispered "*entapai*," meaning "one who has brought shame," when I passed. The men did not whisper; they said it out loud. I wished that Soila—or anyone—was there.

At least my grandfather's wife did not scream at me or beat me. She acted as if I did not exist.

The loneliness and shame were bearable because I knew I would soon go back to school. "Just make it through this day," I told myself.

*　　*　　*

The next time I visited my grandfather, I asked for a year.

"Nice," he said, "we are Maasai. The cut is part of who we are. We cannot put it off forever. How old are you now?"

"Nine. Ten soon."

"Ten," he said. He was quietly thinking to himself. Ten was still on the young side to get the cut.

"Please. I need more time," I said.

"I've already given you time," he said.

"Grandfather," I said, "I want to make you proud. I want to make my father proud. Please let me stay in school. It was my father's dream."

He was silent for a long time. I let him think. "I will give you your year," he said at last. "But not forever."

I nodded. It was all I could ask.

On that visit, my grandfather allowed me to catch a bus to Soila's new town.

It was a small, typical Maasai town, a few houses clustered around the central pen for the animals. The houses were the simple mud and dung structures that would melt back into the earth when people moved to better grazing land. There was no electricity, and the women had to walk for water and wood. Everyone knew one another, and everyone was related by birth or marriage.

Soila's husband was older than she was, and he had another wife and children. Soila was pregnant.

"You can stay," he said to me, "as long as you go back to school soon." He did not speak to me for the rest of my visit.

With her husband at his other wife's home, Soila and I had a couple of days alone.

Her house was tiny, a traditional Maasai home, but as clean and well kept as our mother's had been. She cooked just as well too. I loved boarding school, but this felt like a home. Then I would catch Soila's husband scowling at us as he walked out with his cattle, and I felt like a stranger again.

"Are you going to be okay?" I asked her.

"This is life." She shrugged.

I was more determined than ever that it would not be my life.

The next time my grandfather and I talked about the cut, I asked to put it off indefinitely. "I love school," I said. "I have already gone further than anyone else in the family. Give me the chance to finish."

I no longer had the excuse of being too young. I was almost eleven, a normal age for a girl to get the cut and get married.

But now I had come further in school than any girl we knew.

"What would your parents say?" he asked.

"I think they would be proud of me. What would my father say if he saw his daughter finish primary school?"

My grandfather said nothing.

"What would my father say if his daughter went to high school?"

He said nothing again.

"Please," I said. "If I have an education, I can get a better job. I can help the whole family."

"How could you be a mother and have a job?"

"I can find a way. I have come so far."

He was silent for another minute. "Going to school is a dream, Nice. You are right about that. But what about honoring our traditions?"

"Grandfather," I said, "do I show you respect?"

He smiled. "You've always been a good girl."

"Then please," I said. "Let me do it my way."

He looked at me. I might have been tall like a *twiga,* but I was still skinny like a child.

"You are young still," he said. "You have lost so much."

He nodded to himself as he spoke, almost as if he was convincing himself.

"Every woman wants to marry," he said. "Every woman eventually wants to have children. I will let you decide when you are ready. You will come to your senses."

My grandfather agreed to let me wait as long as I needed to get the cut. I was free to finish school.

Freedom

Soila and I were always different people. She was domestic and serious. I was a tomboy and a dreamer. But until I refused the cut, our personalities would make little difference in the lives we would lead. A Maasai girl gets the cut, marries young, and spends her life taking care of others. Soila would still follow that path.

I had no idea what I would do. I got to stay in school. Beyond that, I wasn't sure what the future held. Some days I pictured myself as a famous model, doing whatever famous models did (try on clothes all day?). Other days, I thought I would be a politician, like my father. I could not imagine talking to strange men, but I could imagine writing important speeches and wearing fancy suits. More often, I thought I would marry a handsome Maasai man who would not mind that I was uncut. He would walk by my side, just as my father had walked with my mother, and tell me I was a great wife. Maybe we would be rich enough to hire a woman to help me with the dishes. My imagination did not run as far as actually picturing a man helping me with the housework. I imagine that little girls everywhere daydream about their lives. It was unusual for a Maasai girl to actually be able to make those daydreams happen.

For the first few months after my grandfather agreed to stand by me, I woke up at small sounds in the night. I imagined that men might come on motorbikes to drag me away to the cut and a waiting husband. I would hide under the covers and close my eyes tight, like any little girl waiting for the monsters to go away. The difference was, my monsters were real, and hiding would not make them go away. They would eat me up and I would disappear.

During the day, I would stay by my teachers, even during breaks. If my uncle and his friends came for me, I needed someone strong by my side. Any time I heard a car or motorbike approaching on the road, I would tense up and look for the best direction to run.

But as the months went by, nothing happened. I realized that even though my grandfather did not agree with me, even though I must have seemed a little crazy to him, he was going to support me. After I had been at school for a few years, he stopped asking me when I planned to get the cut; he just resigned himself to my decision.

I did not realize how much dread was inside me until it was no longer there. Ever since that early morning when my mother had taken me to see the cut, a weight of fear was always in the background of my thoughts. Now the weight was gone, and everything seemed a bit easier, a bit better. I was not going to get the cut. I was free in a way I had never experienced. I did not have to run or make endless excuses to my family. Finally, I had a clear path forward.

Boarding School

Now that I was free, I was exactly where I most wanted to be. I was learning. For wealthy people in the West who take education for granted, it is hard to understand how joyous the freedom to learn is. I threw myself into my studies and vowed to take advantage of every opportunity.

I am not saying it was easy. I missed my brothers and sisters, my grandfather, and my friends back home. Our teachers guided us, gave us discipline, but a teacher, no matter how caring, is not family. I smiled when the teachers praised me, and they did take time to praise the girls. But they had lives and families of their own. I spent hours with Miss Caroline, but even she had other girls to teach and two children of her own to take care of, and I could not always see her when I wanted. There were far more girls hungry for attention than teachers to go around.

Sometimes I would forget for just a moment that I could not run to Soila whenever I wanted. I would get a good grade on a test, or a teacher would praise an essay, and I would smile about how proud Soila would be when I showed her. When I remembered that I would not see Soila anytime soon, probably for months, my smile would disappear. This was in the days before cell phones were common, and Soila lived in a traditional home without a landline. When I was not physically with her, we could not speak at all. Each time I remembered how far away she was, I would feel the fresh pain of that loss.

I did not have a mother to sing me to sleep at night, and I would wake up clutching my pillow, whimpering for a kind touch. I longed for Soila to stroke my hair and help me get back to sleep. Even when one is surrounded by other girls, a school dormitory can feel like a very lonely place.

In some ways, we girls had to become our own families. I was in primary school until about age fourteen and high school until about age eighteen. We girls were together all that time. We grew up without a mother's guidance, so we did what we could to help one another. Some girls knew how to braid or style hair, and they would help the rest of us keep ourselves neat. When another girl's hands were on my head, I would close my eyes and imagine Soila plaiting my hair. (I had conveniently forgotten that Soila would really yank on my scalp as she worked.) Those who knew how to sew would teach the others how to affix buttons or let out the hems of our uniforms. There was always a smart girl with a great memory who could help the rest of us with our English spelling, since it made absolutely no sense. This was not like having a mother or a beloved aunty, but it was a comfort.

When I started menstruating, I knew what to do because I had seen my fellow students handle their flows. Feminine hygiene products were expensive and hard to get, and girls in my part of Kenya had to improvise. Back home, a woman might use a bit of fur or cloth, or she might go without. A lot of women simply stayed close to home when their periods came. At boarding school, we had foam mattresses in our dorm rooms. During her time of the month, a girl would tear off a small piece of that foam and use it to absorb the bleeding. As the years went by, each girl's mattress would grow smaller and smaller. The mattress might be less comfortable, but at least she could stay in school and not worry about bloodstains.

When I first noticed a few drops of blood on my underwear, I did not panic. I did what I had seen the other girls do. It was hardly an ideal solution, but it did the job.

Even with the other girls helping me, there were nights when I would push my head into my pillow, hiding my tears. But as I grew older, I did not think of home as much. I no longer followed my teachers around looking for attention. I was busy with my work. The girls around me were friends, not strangers.

I tried to befriend all my fellow students and usually succeeded, but some girls were special. My friend Irene was Luhya, one of the larger ethnic groups in Kenya. Unlike the Maasai, the Luhya don't practice FGM. We did not talk much about the cut because I did not like to dwell on the bad parts of home, but she knew I had run away. On those nights when I could not sleep, worried that my uncles would hunt me down, she would whisper, "Do not worry, Nice. I am here. No one will get you."

We shared our food, and we traded clothes. I taught her Maasai songs, and she made me laugh with stories about her little brothers and sisters.

I sometimes went home with her on holiday breaks. Even though Irene and I were both Kenyan, our homes were different. Her family lived in a concrete-block house, and though looking back I realize it was quite modest, it felt substantial and solid to me at the time. The

Luhya were not people of the cattle: they farmed, mostly, or traveled to the cities and worked there. It felt strange to see men working the soil; it is the wives who tend the gardens at Maasai homes. I helped Irene's mother with the housework and the cooking; if they were going to welcome me into their home, I decided, I was determined not to be a burden. Her parents praised both of us for our hard work and fed us until we were stuffed.

"I'm sorry I cannot take you back home with me," I said to Irene. My half brothers and sisters barely tolerated *me* in their homes. I certainly could not bring them another mouth to feed.

"You have done plenty for me, Nice," she said.

I did not have anything extra to spare for her. What was she talking about?

"You helped me with my essay last week," she said.

"That was easy."

"Hey, for you, maybe. But why do you think I needed the help?"

I was glad. Knowing that I could help made me feel good. Sometimes helping our friends feels like a gift.

"Besides, you do not have to take me somewhere else. This is our home right here."

She was right. Together, the students made a home of sorts.

By the time I was a teenager, I had perfected my English and Swahili; most educated Kenyans are at least bilingual, and those of us who speak minority languages such as Maa are often trilingual. One morning in English class, my high school teacher asked me, "Nice, would you like to study the computer next year?"

"I would," I answered.

It wasn't a very exciting exchange, and my answer was probably not even true (I have never been very interested in technology), but

I realized suddenly that I had answered without translating. I had not worried about the strange English verb tenses. I had not worried about whether I was using the correct words. I just thought of the answer and gave it.

I spoke English. Really spoke it. When I realized that I could think in all three languages, I grabbed books—any books—and started reading. Even economics seemed fascinating when I could study it in English. I probably could have read an appliance manual—if there were any appliance manuals around—and enjoyed it. So many doors were opening, so many possibilities.

I learned mathematics, history, and all the basics. Because I was living at school, I had the time to really devote myself to study. Housework was something I had found reasons to avoid; the work of learning, on the other hand, was a joy. I did well. I began to realize that I was good at things, and maybe I was not quite as lazy as I had assumed. College had seemed like a far-off dream when I was little, but as the years went by, the possibility became real. My life was opening in ways I had never anticipated.

Money was scarce. I had to work at things I did not enjoy—cleaning clothes, weeding gardens, any part-time job I could find—to afford the work I liked. I never had the necessities: socks without holes, deodorant, and a fresh bar of soap were unheard-of luxuries. I cleaned myself by pushing scraps of soap together to form new bars, and I wrote using pencils so short no one else could grip them properly. I would take hand-me-down clothes from the older girls and then, in turn, pass them on to the younger students.

Girls would notice when others went without. Clothes, toiletries, or school supplies would appear on my bunk. No one took credit. No one wanted to embarrass me. It was always something to make my life easier. It was never much—no one at my school was wealthy—but it seemed like a lot to me.

"My mother sent me too many shoelaces," Irene would say. "Why don't you take a pair?"

I knew she was trying to help me without making it seem like charity, but my laces had become so short with repeated mending that I could barely tie my shoes. I would thank her and accept whatever was being offered. There was no reason to be proud. It was through these little kindnesses that those of us with less were able to make it through school. My parents had given to others when they could, and I knew that someday I might be able to do the same for someone else.

It was not just the girls who helped. I barely had enough money for school fees. When I was late with payments, the school gave me a little extra time. Sometimes even that help wasn't enough, and I would take time off to earn more money. When I came back, there was always a place waiting for me, and my teachers would help me catch up academically. At the end, I owed a bit of money to the school, and they let me graduate anyway. We took care of one another.

In my memories, it is not the things I did not have that stand out, but what I did have. Teachers who made sure we learned. A safe place to grow. Girls who shared what little they had to make sure that everyone had enough. It was fun to learn from one another, to share what we had to benefit everyone.

I am not saying it was always peace and bliss. Girls teased one another, had rivalries, fought over petty things. We were human, and we were young. We were a sort of family, but every family has its squabbles. In the end, the good outweighed the bad.

For the first time, I saw girls grow up and get jobs or go to college, something that simply had not happened where I grew up. Occasionally in Kimana, a boy would go off to the big city, but never a woman. College was something for Europeans or rich people in Nairobi, not village girls. But my classmates at boarding school were not wealthy foreigners; they were rural Kenyan girls like me. It was with their minds, and their cleverness, that they survived. If they could do it, I realized, so could I.

A Different Path

As the years passed for me at boarding school, Soila settled into life in her new town. All the important choices in her life had been made, and her role was now wife.

Even her body was no longer hers. Within five years, she had given birth to three children, all boys. She was still a teenager—a child herself in much of the world—but she was responsible for babies of her own.

Her life, like our mother's, became one of constant work: caring for three little ones, feeding her family, tending her garden, cleaning her home. Unlike my mother's marriage, though, Soila's was not based on love but on duty. My mother worked hard, but she also knew the joy of a partnership. She could take pleasure in knowing she made her husband happy. He smiled at her, touched her gently, complimented her cooking. She knew that her work was valued and that she was valued. When my parents walked, they walked side by side. When Soila walked, like most Maasai women, she was expected to stay several paces behind her husband. In a joyless marriage, the work was simply drudgery.

Her one piece of happiness was her three boys. They were beautiful, and even had they not been, they would have been beautiful in her eyes. She sang the songs that a Maasai mother sings about her boys: how strong they are, how brave they are, how quick and clever they are.

I visited Soila on a school break when I was about thirteen. I stirred the cornmeal into the water for the *ugali* while she trimmed her eldest son's hair. Her baby slept in a sling on her back. The third child played in the dirt beside us.

"Such beautiful boys," I said.

"Yes," she said. "I wish we could stop at three."

I was a young teen, but I had been reading and talking to the other girls at school.

"You could stop," I said.

"You think my husband is going to leave me alone?" Soila laughed. "You will learn differently when you get married."

"There is birth control," I said.

Soila was silent for a moment. "You should not know about such things."

"I am not using it, Soila. But I have learned. There is nothing wrong with learning."

"My husband is not going to do that."

"He does not have to know."

I explained that there were forms of birth control that no one— not even her husband—could see. Few Maasai women discuss birth control, even among themselves, but at school, pamphlets and health care information were widely available, and sometimes speakers would come and teach us. I had access to knowledge that the women back home did not. Talking about birth control might not have been modest, but it was too important a subject for me to keep quiet about. I knew that Soila could take control of her reproductive life. And I knew that Kimana had a small medical facility.

Soila made an excuse to go into town—with the work she did selling vegetables, it was more than believable. She was right that her husband would never have agreed to birth control, but fortunately, she did not need his permission to use it, and at the clinic she was able to get an injection to prevent pregnancy. If she could sneak off occasionally to the doctor, she would never have to have another child. She would not be worn-out from multiple births, stooped and exhausted by the time she was twenty-five. She would not have to worry about feeding too many mouths. She could focus on making life as good as possible for her three boys.

It was a treasure, that small amount of power she got from controlling her own body. It was a treasure to commit an act of defiance, even though her husband would never know what she had done. It was something for Soila to cling to.

Even with all the work she was doing for her own family, Soila took time for me. Our visits were brief. I was at boarding school, and getting to her home was difficult. She was a mother and could not leave her family to see me, even if her husband had given permission.

She would give me what money she could put together. All I had to offer were stories about my life.

"Anna sneaks out to meet her boyfriend, and she thinks no one notices her buttons all messed up when she comes back," I said.

"I thought you boarding school girls were supposed to be smart. Do not let me catch you doing any of that nonsense," Soila said.

"You do not have to worry about me." I knew that flirting with boys was not going to help me finish school.

I read to her from my English textbook.

"You sound like a *mzungu*," she said, using the Swahili word for a white foreigner.

"Thank you."

"I did not say that was a compliment."

I laughed; I knew she was proud of me. Soila had never learned much English, and I was fluent. I told her about my classes, about which teachers were the best. We talked about history, science, and math.

She mothered me, telling me to comb my hair, to put lotion on my dry skin, to keep my uniform cleaner and straighter. I would pretend I was bothered, but it felt good to have someone who cared enough about my life to nag. I still drove her crazy by going off into my own little world when there was housework to be done, but her scolding felt almost like a homecoming.

I loved watching her sons crawl, take their first steps, smile at me. I loved the feeling of their tiny little fingers grasping on to mine and their beautiful baby smell. Soila was a typical Maasai mother, loving but tough. Like my mother, she did not tolerate nonsense. I was free to be a doting aunt, clapping at her children's small accomplishments, listening to them prattle, and generally letting them get away with murder. Like my father, I would just happen to have a little candy in my pockets when the children were around. Soila would tut at me and tell me I was ruining their teeth, but I saw her secret smile. Soila and I both loved those little boys, and I marveled as they shot up between my visits.

But those visits were few and far between, and when I was away, I did not hear from Soila. Today cell phones are common in even the smallest Maasai towns. Back then, though, I did not have a way to talk with her when I wasn't with her. I missed her voice. I missed my family. And I know that she missed me too.

The truth was, she was stuck, and I was drifting away.

First Steps

I did not want other girls to have to be like Soila, to have their possibilities shut down while they were still children.

But what could I do? The idea of helping girls in my community was as audacious as my father's plan to help the Maasai. Who would listen to me? I was *entapai,* a girl who had brought shame to her family. For years, my own family would not speak to me; Soila was my only friend back home.

When I was fourteen and moved up to high school, I decided it was time to try to convince other girls to run.

When I approached girls gathered outside their homes, they would pretend I was not there. I would try to walk with them when they collected wood or water for their mothers, but they would speed up and change direction every time I got near. I would try to talk to them after church, and they would just roll their eyes and walk away. For a year, I tried on every break, and every break, I failed.

My breakthrough came because of clothes. My boarding school uniform was a skirt and a blouse—real grown-up clothes. Girls in my town did not go beyond elementary education, and their uniforms were childish-looking dresses with big collars.

"Would you like to wear this?" I said to them one day, twirling in the skirt for effect.

They still did not speak to me, and they certainly did not say yes, but I could see the interest in their faces. Nagging can get boring, but many young girls are interested in looking grown-up as soon as possible.

Parents told their girls not to talk to me; I was a bad influence. Fortunately, girls do not always listen to everything adults tell them.

"Fine, I will talk to you," one said. "As long as nobody sees."

A few others nodded their heads yes.

"But," the girl who had spoken said, "we are not staying long."

We met under the shade of a tree outside of town. I told them about school, about the freedom I had there. I told them I did not have to walk miles fetching water or sticks for my mother. I did not have to carry my younger siblings on my hip. I could read and no one would tell me to stop. If I wanted, I could stay up talking all night with a friend—not that I actually did that, but I could.

I did not tell them not to get the cut. Instead, I asked them what they wanted in life. It is not a question they were used to. Their lives were already set because they were girls. They would learn their duties from their mothers, get the cut, and, as young teenagers, become mothers themselves.

Some of the girls wanted to drive buses full of tourists. Some thought they could teach young children. Some wanted to be park rangers. They did not dream of being doctors, professors, or politicians; their crazy dreams were just regular jobs to the men around them. Their dreams were small, but they felt nearly impossible.

"Do you think you can do those things and get the cut?" I asked.

I could see their faces opening up, the possibilities lighting up their eyes. It is no wonder the parents did not want their daughters talking to me. I was an example. That is why I was dangerous.

"Think about it while I'm gone," I said. "I will come up with a plan."

I went back to school. For the next couple of months, I tried to think of a way to help the girls escape. I had no home of my own and no money to spare. When I was in our town, I lived with my half brothers and sisters. My siblings barely tolerated me; they would not have wanted to hide girls in their home and risk their reputations. They were poor young people living with a crazy *entapai;* they did not need to encourage more hostility from the neighbors.

I visited Aunty Grace and told her I wanted girls to escape FGM. "They can stay here," she said. "It is my duty as a Christian."

Aunty Grace lived far enough away from our town that no one would think to look there, at least for a few days. It was not a long-term solution. Once people figured out that she was sheltering girls, they would pressure her to stop. There might be violence, but at least for a while, the girls would have somewhere to go.

The next time I came home, seven girls were willing to talk to me. I told them about Aunty Grace and how she had once sheltered me. With her help, I could give them time to talk to their families.

"There is a possibility," I told them, "that you do not have to get the cut."

It would not be like the time I had run. They would not have to escape during the darkness. They would not start running minutes before the ceremony. Instead, when they went out to get water, they would keep walking and not come back.

No one was ready to escape, but the girls said they would think about it.

I went back to school. By my next break, five of the seven girls had decided they wanted to escape FGM. Two of the five said that their mothers were sympathetic—while the cut is expected of Maasai women, that does not mean all of them want it for their own daughters. Those girls told their parents about me, and how I was succeeding at boarding school. They did not have to slip away.

Three girls ran.

The people in town suspected I was behind their escape. We had been quiet, but people had noticed me trying to talk to girls. For them to run was too much of a coincidence.

That evening, relatives of the girls came to my half siblings' home, where they knew I was staying during my school break. "Where are they?" they asked me at the door. "What have you done to them?"

I was a skinny teenage girl. The relatives were all men, all larger and stronger than me. I did not answer.

"Come outside," one of the men said.

My half brother pushed me aside. He stood in front of the door. He had not spoken to me since I had refused to get the cut.

"You want to see this woman? You see me first," he said.

The men slowly began to walk away. When they were gone, I thanked my brother. He nodded but said nothing to me in return. I shut the door.

I did not want my community against me. But I knew I had to save our girls. I had to find a better way.

Amref

In that first group of seven, two girls were cut, two convinced their families to let them stay in school, and three ran away. The runaways eventually convinced their families not to make them get the cut or found shelter in other homes.

I was not the only person fighting for girls. There were special schools that took in girls escaping FGM (something I wish I had known about when I ran). There were teachers at boarding schools—women like my English teacher Miss Caroline—who provided shelter for girls. There were NGOs working to stop the cut altogether. But those people and resources were not everywhere. In my town, I was the only person fighting.

Every time I went home, I talked to more girls. I did not have huge successes—just a girl here and a girl there—but I felt I was making progress. It did not always go smoothly. Once I had to hide a girl under my bed while her family searched our house for her. But we were moving forward.

When I was about sixteen, I was talking with some girls when a man named Peter from the African Medical and Research

Foundation (Amref) first saw me. Amref is an organization working for health care advances in Africa. Here I was, a girl still in school, without a degree of any kind, without any expert knowledge, and I was making a small difference. Peter noticed. If I had the courage to speak up, maybe I was someone Amref could work with.

He went to the elders and asked if I could work with him.

Amref had previously approached the elders in our community in hopes of finding a boy and a girl to teach our young people about health. None of the village girls had gone past elementary school, and even if they had, the elders would never have allowed them to get training. A girl should be modest, quiet, and, most of all, obedient. A girl teaching others would be none of those things, and talk about contraception, prenatal care, and the prevention of sexually transmitted diseases—a necessary part of health education—could corrupt her. The elders had rejected Amref's offer.

In spite of that rejection, the elders knew that Amref had something to offer. AIDS and other sexually transmitted diseases were a problem that our people were aware of but did not discuss. Vaccinations could prevent diseases in our children and our elderly. Hygiene and nutrition advice could prevent diseases and improve health. The elders wanted people to have that knowledge, and, with Amref's help, the elders knew that people could learn. Peter told the elders that I could be the girl teacher, and this time the elders agreed. I was *entapai*. Allowing me to get the training would not ruin me because I was already ruined.

Along with a young man named Douglas, I received the training. Like me, Douglas was in high school. Even though Douglas was not the first boy from our community to attend school, it was still an accomplishment. Education was a struggle for all Maasai, male and female.

Douglas was tall and thin, a typical Maasai young man. But he was not typical. He was determined to go to college. He was determined to make positive change. And unlike most Maasai men, he was willing to work alongside a woman as a colleague. Amref drove the two of us to training sessions. There, pairs of teens from throughout my part of Kenya heard speakers who talked to us about preventive health care, hygiene, infectious diseases, and empowering women. They gave us pamphlets to read and take home. The speakers were excited, and while listening to them, I got excited. Yes, there was even more to be done than I had ever suspected, but, as I listened to the Amref trainers, I thought that change seemed possible.

Amref wanted us to learn to host community youth groups. Girls and boys would meet together and learn about health, and then they would go home and teach their elders. I knew that youth groups would never work in my community. Parents would never let their children attend coed meetings. But even though that specific plan would not work for us, the information Amref provided was good. They taught us to lead meetings. Taught us how to get discussions started and how to direct conversations. They taught us about birth control, vaccinations, improving water and sanitation, and making childbirth safer.

They taught us where to go to find solutions to local problems. NGOs, private enterprise, and the Kenyan government offered assistance with some of the issues we faced, but if the people did not know where to get that help, it did no good.

As just one example, periods can cause a huge disruption in Kenyan girls' lives, but sanitary products are rarely available and, when they are, prohibitively expensive. Women improvised, just as we had at school with our foam mattresses. There are better solutions, though. Through Amref I learned about Afripads, reusable sanitary products. These are simple absorbent cloth pads, sewn by women in Africa, that button around the underwear. Women soak, wash, and reuse them many times. Where Afripads are available, they have made a tremendous impact: absences from school for girls who receive them go down as much as 44 percent. No one in my town knew about them, though, until Amref provided the knowledge and I shared it with my community.

The elders expected me to help improve basic health care; I do not think they considered that avoiding FGM was part of that basic improvement. I already knew that the cut was painful, but I had much to learn about how dangerous it was. When a girl bled to death or got an infection from the cut, people said she was cursed or had another illness. I learned how the infections came from unsterile conditions. A girl's body could go into shock from the cut, and if it was left untreated (and there would be no treatment), she could die. I learned that the cut could cause fatal hemorrhaging. I learned that even if the girl survives the initial procedure, she can develop, among many other problems, cysts, abscesses, and lifelong urinary incontinence and have chronic pain during sex. Complications from repeated infections could cause infertility. Some women can have complications during childbirth. I was already against the cut; the training showed me how much worse the procedure was than I had imagined.

The Maasai had seen the negative outcomes of FGM, but there had always been excuses and explanations. I now had the science to show them that those excuses were unacceptable. Armed with my new knowledge, I convinced a few more girls to avoid the cut. Not many, and certainly not enough, but a few. I realized that I could make a difference. I ended up volunteering with Amref the entire time I was in high school. I decided to be the first in my family to attend college, and then I would use my knowledge to work for the Maasai. I was going to fight to make sure every girl had a chance. I had found my calling.

A Bus Ride That Changed
Everything

I knew that if I wanted to work with NGOs to help the Maasai, I would need an education. I graduated from high school when I was about eighteen, and I decided to go to college. I was not sure how a person went about picking or enrolling in a school. No other girls in my area had been to college. Very few boys in the surrounding area had either. No one in my family had stayed in school past the elementary level. In North America and Europe, teenagers can look at college standings, research online, and ask their school counselors. I did not know how to do any of that. People from educated families can ask their parents, or at least some relative or neighbor. I had no one to ask.

So I took my chances and boarded a bus for Nairobi. I had a small bag with a few clothes, the first cell phone I ever owned, and all the money I had managed to save up—enough, I hoped, for tuition and space on a bed. I said a little prayer, hoping that I was doing the right thing.

The bus was crowded and warm. The windows were open, and though that cooled things off a bit, it also let in the dust. The road to Nairobi had not been paved. What is now a three-hour journey would take us all day.

"Sit here," said a soldier, motioning toward the empty seat next to him. I hesitated, unsure of whether I should sit next to a strange man. But it was a long ride, the bus was crowded, and he seemed safe.

We sat silently for a while, but then we hit a huge pothole and I gasped.

"Do you feel well?" he asked.

"Just a little bumpy," I said, laughing at myself.

"You get used to it," he said. "It's better than the Nairobi traffic."

I relaxed a bit. "Do you go to Nairobi often?"

"Too often," he said. "But it has its good points. Why are you going?"

"College," I said.

"Where?"

I was embarrassed to admit that I had not picked a school. From his uniform, I could tell he was an officer, so I knew he had some education. I took a deep breath and decided that sitting next to him must not be a coincidence. "To be honest," I said, "I could use some help."

On the long ride to Nairobi—he was not wrong about the traffic—we talked about my ambitions. I wanted to spend my life working to help the Maasai, and especially Maasai women, get ahead.

"You need to go to the Kenya Institute of Management," he said. "When we arrive, let me take you there."

He walked me from the bus station to the school, about a half hour's walk. He even called a few friends to try to find me some roommates. I thanked him, but he told me it was no trouble. I knew that was not true; he had spent an entire day helping a clueless country girl. "Just do well in school," he said as he left.

I never saw him again, so I was never able to return the favor, but I will always be grateful.

If he had not helped me, I don't know what I would have done. I used the advice of a complete stranger to make one of the biggest decisions of my life. I shake my head when I think about how crazy and naive I was. I followed a stranger through an unfamiliar city. Maybe God was looking out for me. Maybe I just got lucky and found a well-meaning and informed man. But I made the right decision.

I went into the main office and asked how I could enroll. The answer was paperwork. Lots of paperwork. I spent hours that day and the next in the office, filling out forms and then reading them two or three times to make sure my answers were correct. None of the questions were particularly difficult, but I did not want to be rejected on a technicality.

Every hour or so, I would go back to the receptionist and ask for her help; I could tell from her patience that I was not the first person from a small town who had come in clueless. "Do not worry," she said when I finally handed over the completed stack of papers. "It just gets easier from here."

And just like that, I was the first person in my family to enroll in college.

Nairobi

I had been to Nairobi with my father when I was a child, but being there on my own, without an adult's hand to guide me, was a new experience. Back home, a three-story building was a skyscraper; Nairobi had great glass towers and housing developments full of thousands of people. I saw my first female driver on the streets of Nairobi, and she seemed at ease—bored, even, as if she was doing something completely normal. I stood staring, mouth open, at the sight. Then I noticed dozens of women behind the wheel and realized it was in fact completely normal.

Back home, I recognized everyone I passed, and walking took a while because I would have to stop and chat with several people along the way. Nairobi was a city of strangers. I quickly learned that if you spoke to a person passing by, they thought you were crazy. I heard dozens of languages in the streets, but rarely someone speaking Maa. Daily, I saw more people than I was likely to meet back home in a lifetime, but I had never been so alone.

There was possibility in Nairobi, but also danger. You had to keep anything valuable tucked away in a pocket or hidden under your shirt. Acres of slums nestled against gated communities full of spacious air-conditioned homes. I had to get used to buying my milk from a supermarket in a heavily guarded shopping mall rather than getting it straight from the cow. I had to learn to ignore the litter and the dirt. There was barbed wire and a security check at the entrance to every building. I learned that living in the big city meant paying for everything from a spot on a mattress to the water you drank, and usually paying too much.

I had not planned for how very expensive a large city can be. I had struggled to pay my boarding school fees, but Nairobi cost even more. With that soldier's help, I found a room with two other girls in a home in Land Mawe, and the three of us shared one bed and a small cooker. Land Mawe is not quite a slum, but it is a poor area. People live close together. You have to watch your things all the time or they will get up and wander away. I hand washed my clothes and hung them up in the sun. One day I decided to go home and study while my skirt and blouse dried. Who would take wet laundry? I found out that someone would, so I had to make do with even less to wear than the little I had brought.

I did not last long in that rental. Even though the area was relatively cheap, I could not afford it. The pavement quickly wore out my shoes. The milk cost three to four times what it cost at home. A bag of cornmeal to make *ugali* could easily take my budget for the week. If someone had found a way to make us pay for air, I am sure they would have charged for that too. I did not have my rent one week, and then another, and the other girls asked me to leave. They were struggling too, and they could not afford to cover my part of the rent.

I knew that a young man from my town was living nearby. We were in the same clan, so in a way we were family. I asked for his help finding something I could afford. I told him how scared I was. I had heard stories about what can happen to a girl alone in Nairobi.

"You're staying with us," he said.

He rented a small room with two other men, both Maasai from our area; they shared a single bed and a small burner to cook their food. Staying with three unmarried men was a huge risk. I know it scandalized my family—the idea scandalized me. I still cannot quite believe I did it. But I trusted them. In that giant, lonely city, they were as close as I had to family. They barely had enough for themselves, but they knew I had nowhere else to go.

Somehow, the four of us managed to live in that small room. I took the bed at night while they slept on a thin roll-out mattress on the floor. I offered to take the floor, but they absolutely refused. They strung up a sheet so I could have some privacy.

Whenever I earned money, I gave it to them. I cooked for them, helped clean their clothes—making sure to wait while they dried— and did anything I could think of to earn my keep. But I knew they were helping me far more than I was helping them. Together, the four of us managed to build a little bit of home in that big, frightening city. It was not always comfortable, and we sometimes got on one another's nerves, but we were safe.

My school was miles across the city from our neighborhood. Anything closer was too expensive. Back home, most people traveled with their feet. Nairobi was loud, with cars honking in the constant traffic jams. There is no public transportation and the city is spread out. The *matatus*, private buses often decorated with bright, graffiti-like paint jobs depicting everything from superheroes to Bob Marley to Bible verses, are packed. Minibike drivers hire out a perch on the back of their seats to people in a hurry who want to zip around the bigger cars. The riders clutch the drivers and pray they can balance on a few inches of seat.

I could not afford a ride on a motorbike, much less a taxi. I did not know any *matatu* routes, and even had I known any, I was frightened of squeezing on with a bunch of strangers. In the tight quarters of the buses, men's hands find their way onto women's bodies.

I decided that my feet were the best option, and the only one I could afford.

"If you get lost," my roommate said, "look for the green color of the Afya Centre and you will know where to go."

I followed that building like a beacon. I am sure I walked miles out of my way, but it kept me from getting lost.

One evening a man approached me on my walk home.

"Excuse me, madam, do you have a minute?" he said.

He was dressed in a suit and tie, his shoes beautifully shined even in the Nairobi dirt. His English was perfect. I decided it was okay to talk to him.

"I work for a modeling agency, and I couldn't help noticing you. Could we talk?" He handed me a card embossed with his name and the name of an agency. People had always called me *karembo*, or beautiful, so I admit I was a little vain about my looks. When I was a little girl I had dreamed about being a model. Maybe that dream could come true.

He suggested that we go to a hotel restaurant downtown, and we walked there together. "Order anything you want," he said when we sat down.

As we sat drinking tea and eating *mendazi*, a kind of fried bun, he showed me pictures of beautiful women he represented. His clients had been featured on billboards and in magazine spreads and even television ads. If I agreed to let him represent me, he said, I could be working in a week. All he had to do was make a quick call to the office, and I would be on my way to fame and money.

"Oh no: my phone's dead. Can I borrow yours?"

I handed over my phone. He went outside to make a call.

I sat for a few minutes, already spending money in my head. I would get an apartment in the city. I would invite Soila and her children there and buy them clothes and shiny toys. Maybe I could even be one of those women who drive a car.

I waited a few more minutes. I looked out the door, and I did not see the man. Maybe he had gone somewhere with better reception. I waited a bit longer. He did not come back.

I started to get a sick feeling in my stomach.

I had no cash. I did not have my phone to call anyone for help, and who would I have called? No one I knew could afford to pay the bill at a hotel restaurant.

I was going to get arrested for stealing, I thought. I could not think of what to do. I sat there for three hours.

I started to cry. The waiter walked up to my table.

"Was the *mendazi* that bad?" he said.

I told him the story. He put a hand on my shoulder and listened, nodding.

"Welcome to Nairobi," he said.

I nodded. "I cannot pay," I said, "but I can come back. I can get the money."

He shook his head. "I will take care of it if you promise never to follow a stranger anywhere again."

I thanked him. There were kind people in this city. I had lost my phone, but it could have been worse. I had followed a strange man to a hotel. I left the restaurant ashamed but unhurt.

When I was following the man to the hotel, I had not paid attention to where we were going. I had lost sight of the Afya Centre, and I had no idea where I was. I was afraid to ask for help or directions. I did not know who I could trust and who would rob me. I wandered for hours.

Finally, I saw the green paint of the Afya Centre, and it was absolutely the most beautiful color I had ever seen. I was on the wrong side, and I was miles out of the way, but I cried with relief. I finally crawled into bed late that night, my feet covered with blisters. My roommates were upset; they had been frightened when I was so late. *At least I am safe,* I thought, *and at least someone cares whether I get home safely.*

I managed somehow. I acclimated to the crowds. Once I learned the neighborhoods, I stopped getting lost. After a while, I did not even need to use the Afya Centre to navigate.

I will never be a city person at heart, but I got used to it, and I learned to love certain parts of Nairobi. It is full of strangers, but it is also full of dear friends from all ethnicities, not just Maasai. Once I stopped being afraid of how massive everything was, I learned to appreciate the beautiful buildings and the youthful energy. I still love milk fresh from the cow, but I also love an Indian roti or a French pastry. Most of all, I learned to appreciate how much opportunity there is in a city. Large multinational corporations, NGOs from all over the world, and the Kenyan government are all in Nairobi. If I wanted progress for myself and my people, I was in the right place.

On my breaks from school, though, I loved coming home. On

the bus back, even in the famous Kenyan traffic, I would feel my shoulders unclenching, my jaw loosening, the knot leaving my stomach. Yes, I was *entapai,* a person who brings shame. Yes, older people shook their heads when I passed, and younger people avoided me as if my status was contagious. But I could relax when I was home. No crowds. No need to worry if people were sizing me up to rob me. Clean air and blessed quiet. Even the "wait awhile" thornbushes were welcome after living on the Nairobi concrete. Well, maybe not welcome, but at least familiar.

Since the night my grandfather's wife beat me and mocked my parents for dying of AIDS, I had been living with my half brothers and sisters. For a while, after I refused the cut, they had allowed me to stay but wouldn't talk to me. As time went by, there were a few words exchanged, and then a few smiles. Now that I was in college, they were proud, and we talked and laughed together as we had as children. I usually managed to buy something for them in Nairobi. It would be small, but my brothers and sisters would smile when I brought out a couple of new spoons or a packet of candy.

They lived a traditional Maasai life, marrying young, having children. None of them finished high school, much less college. As their families grew, they expanded into different houses, but they lived close together. Their children played and watched out for one another. They shared meals and housework.

My uncle's children, on the other hand, had grown up with plenty of money. They never went hungry. They had clean clothes and comfortable beds. As they grew older, they started drinking and taking drugs. One by one, they dropped out of school. The money my uncle had taken from the *harambee* never educated anyone.

Later, my half siblings made decent lives for themselves. They were far from wealthy, but they had a place to shelter and enough to eat. When I came back to visit, it felt like a home. Their houses might have been a little rough around the edges, but they were filled with happiness. It turns out there could be a place for a Maasai who ran from the cut.

Another Loss

I said that my half siblings built their lives together, but that's not entirely true. My father had five children with his first wife. Only three stayed home. One of my half sisters, Mary, wasn't with them. She had the cut, but when my uncle tried to arrange her marriage, she refused.

Refusing to marry the man your family picks does not make a Maasai girl an *entapai,* but it does give her a poor reputation. Like refusing the cut, it takes courage. Male relatives want to marry away girls to gain a dowry. Your family will beat you, shun you, load you down with extra work—whatever it takes to make you obey. In spite of the punishment, Mary still refused. She must have had some of my father's spirit in her.

She met a soldier. He was young and handsome. He was not Maasai. He offered no dowry. The family did not approve. She wanted to be with him anyway.

When he was transferred to another part of the country, she followed him.

I do not know what her life was like with him. I was at boarding school, and it was hard to stay in touch. I heard from my brothers and sisters that she was pregnant with twins. I like to imagine she was happy. I like to imagine she was proud to become a mother. I like to imagine she was in love.

Then she contracted malaria.

Malaria is common in Kenya. NGOs and the government use insecticide to reduce the mosquito population. They give out sleeping nets and encourage people to use them. They administer antimalarial drugs in especially high-risk areas, such as the coastal region and the shores of Lake Victoria, to prevent malaria during pregnancy. These efforts have made the prevalence of the disease decline, but it is still a threat.

Pregnant women have less of an immunity to malaria, and when they do contract the disease, the consequences are greater. They are at risk of illness, anemia, and even death, and their babies are at risk as well.

I knew all this from my work with Amref. If I had been with Mary, I could have shared my knowledge with her. I could have made sure she slept under an insecticide-treated net. I could have made sure she got antimalarial drugs. I could have helped her find NGOs and government programs to assist her.

But she was far away, and no one was there to help. I do not know what precautions, if any, she took. I do not know if she reached out for help from others. I cannot ask her now. She died in childbirth, along with her twin babies.

When I heard the news, I rocked back and forth and cried. *I failed her,* I thought. *I could have saved her.* Another family member had slipped away while I was somewhere else.

But I couldn't have helped, of course. I had just started college. I could barely support myself. I could not solve a problem that affects millions of women. I had to tell myself over and over that I could not have been with her. That I could not change the past.

Back home, my brothers and sisters mourned. When I saw them next, we cried again together. Seeing one another's faces reminded us of the one who was missing.

We were more determined to stay together, to build a life for ourselves. Life had taken too many family members too young. It was up to us to keep going.

Change at Home

After starting college, I still came home whenever I had the time and bus fare. And I kept talking to girls. As more girls saw their friends and family members refuse the cut, it got easier to get girls to talk to me. But I was still having to work with girls one at a time, and there was only one Nice to do the work. If I was going to make a bigger difference, I would have to fight against Maasai support of FGM more broadly.

FGM as it is practiced among the Maasai robs a woman of sexual pleasure and can rob her of her life. There are other forms of FGM throughout the world. Some people make only a small incision or burn on the clitoris. In other cultures, not only the external clitoris but also the inner labia is removed. In still other cultures, the vaginal opening is sewn shut, leaving only a tiny hole. Before her wedding, a girl suffering this form of FGM will have to have a second cut, reopening the vagina.

The roughly two hundred million women worldwide who have had some form of FGM have suffered differently, and their people have cut them for different reasons. But all forms of FGM have one thing in common: they limit and control women's lives. I had seen those limits in my own family. I had seen those limits in Soila's life.

A girl who gets the cut is a girl whose body is no longer her own. I did not fully understand this fact when I ran. I knew only that I did not want to drop out of school and get married. But now, as a college student who had gone through Amref training, I knew exactly what FGM did to girls. It caused pain, permanent injury, and even death. But it did more. It helped cement women in their place as baby makers and servants. It took away their future.

This is the reason that I did not want to replace FGM with something less openly harmful. It is possible to perform FGM in a clinical setting, and to make only a small incision rather than removing the clitoris. In a sterile environment, with the benefit of antibiotics, the health risks are far lower. And if the cut is ceremonial only, a woman might not even lose sexual pleasure. But even if she does not lose her health and pleasure, a woman getting FGM is still losing her autonomy. FGM, even the more innocuous kind, inevitably leads to marriage, and marriage, in those cultures that practice FGM, leads to an erasing of women.

Girls who receive the cut drop out of school. They give up their careers. They work—probably harder than they worked before—but only for the benefit of their families. I have not studied every single community where FGM is practiced. There are far too many. But in every one that I have studied, this relationship holds true.

Because FGM is so intimately tied to early marriage and bearing children, it also affected boys. An unmarried man has no place in the Maasai community. Children were considered a form of wealth, and a man without them was hardly a man at all. Men supported FGM, thinking it created more eligible girls. But men cannot get an education if they have to support a family, so, like girls, they tended to drop out of school early.

The practice depended upon and impacted the whole community. Mothers taught their daughters about the cut, warned them of the consequences of not getting it, and told the fathers when their daughters were ready. Fathers organized and paid for the ceremony, chose spouses for their daughters, and received dowries from the grooms' families. Young men wanted a wife they could trust to stay home, raise children, and have babies; they insisted that only a woman who was cut was good enough. Everyone saw FGM as central to our identity as Maasai, a practice that held us together even though we were a minority in our own country. Without all these groups agreeing to end FGM, there would always be support for the practice.

Kenya declared FGM illegal in 2011, while I was in college. Laws made little difference. The Maasai tend to live in isolated settlements, far from federal oversight. Where the reach of the law was a threat, the Maasai began to get the cut in secret. Instead of getting the cut as part of a community ceremony, the girl was cut at home, with only her closest family members to support her. When outsiders asked the Maasai if they still practiced FGM, they denied it. But in private, the cut was still as much of a threat as ever. Laws were not enough. In order to eradicate FGM, change would have to come from the inside.

Visiting home meant continuing my quest to end FGM. Although the elders had allowed me to train with Amref and a few girls were willing to listen, I realized that I could not make a real difference without reaching all our people. My job was not to save a handful of girls, I realized. It was to change the Maasai way of thinking.

* * *

I had had some success with the girls, so I began talking to their mothers. Tuesday was market day, and I would be waiting by the vendors. Talking to the mothers was similar to talking to the girls. I needed to know the mothers' hopes and fears before I could work with them. Making change, for me, began with asking questions: What do you want for your daughters? What do you want for your family? What does FGM do to help those dreams come true?

The mothers had seen girls die from FGM, though they may not have admitted to themselves that it was the cut that caused death. Armed with my knowledge from Amref, I was able to convince many of them. The bleeding, the fevers, the pain...that is not a curse or a problem with your daughter, I said. It is from the practice itself. They all knew at least one woman, often themselves, who had suffered from the side effects of the procedure. These mothers loved their daughters, and they did not want them to suffer.

Beyond that, I was able to argue the economics. FGM led to early marriage, and early marriage ended a girl's hopes for an education. Education could bring more money for the girl and her family. Mothers struggled to feed and clothe their children, to buy the basic necessities. Early marriage meant more babies. And more babies meant spreading limited resources more thinly. Mothers knew the price of forgoing an education.

They could see my life. They could see that I was the first girl in our village to go to college, and that, even without the cut, I was healthy and happy. No curse had befallen me or my family.

I could convince many women. The problem was the men and, specifically, how they treated me. The men looked at me and saw a woman who was still largely shunned, who was not treated as a grown-up by the men, who was not married and might never have a husband.

If my daughter does not get the cut, they argued, no one will marry her. Her father will shame her. Maybe her future will not be much, but at least she will have a future, a family, a community. Mothers knew the harm that the cut could do, but they feared for their daughters if they did not get it. If I was going to end FGM in my community, I would have to get the men to go along.

I had plenty of patience; talking for months and even years did not scare me. The problem was that I was not allowed to speak to men at all.

I was female, and Maasai women do not lead discussions with men. In fact, they are not expected to participate in discussions at all. Debating was men's work. Worse, I was not just a woman; I was uncut, technically a child. They would turn their backs on me or laugh in my face.

Doing the Work

While in college, I got a part-time job with Amref in Nairobi. I was getting paid for the work I had been doing for years as a volunteer. I finally had money to pay my rent. I tried to find the waiter who had helped me when the man stole my phone, but he was not at the restaurant when I returned. I gave some money to the men who had let me stay with them, but they would not take much. Helping your people was just something you did, they said, not something they expected to be paid for.

"If you want to pay us back," they said, "go out and help someone else."

At least with me gone, the men had a bed to sleep in, so I suppose I gave them that.

Now I had a room that was entirely my own. An entire room. It felt a little strange; except for the nights when I was locked in my grandfather's wife's kitchen, I had never slept alone. It was nice to have a place to study. It was nice to have a clean bed all to myself. It was nice to know I was not making three generous men sleep on a hard floor.

I sent money back to my brothers and sisters. They used it to buy a couple of animals and help with school expenses. Soila was able to buy her sons books.

"I may not be able to give your children fancy things," I told my family, "but I can make sure the next generation gets an education." If our shoes had holes and our clothes were frayed, so be it; we were going to have the things that mattered. It would not be just me moving forward, I determined. It was going to be my entire family together.

More important than my personal dreams, Amref gave me the opportunity to help girls on a larger scale.

My training was an awakening. Amref was flying doctors and nurses into small towns, training midwives and local practitioners, helping communities build or improve water and septic systems and improve oral hygiene and education…after a while, I lost track. There was so much to do, so many projects where Amref was stepping in that I could not keep them straight. My training helped me appreciate the depth and breadth of what was needed in Kenya and what people were doing to achieve those needs.

Some issues I had never considered. I sat in a training session for LGBTQ issues; as far as I knew, I had never met a single gay person before that day, and I did not understand why the training was necessary. From that education, though, I realized that I had met plenty of gay people, but they had not been able to say anything in a culture that does not discuss or even acknowledge homosexuality.

Because Amref is based in Africa and its staff is predominantly African, it is run by individuals who respect and listen to local people. It does not dictate health care solutions from the outside. Instead, it believes in listening to communities and working with all available resources to improve access to and utilization of health care. Amref talks to communities the way that I had talked to the girls back home: by listening first, by addressing individual needs.

Seeing what Amref was doing, I wanted to be a part of it. I had convinced a few girls to avoid the cut. With Amref's training and resources behind me, I knew I could convince whole communities. I was a young college student; I was idealistic and optimistic. I knew in my core that I could make a difference. If my father, a shoeless boy, could help the Maasai move forward, so could I. I was not perfect, but I was determined.

Luckily, the leaders at Amref saw some ability within me as well. Looking back, I was inexperienced—horribly so. I was naive; I had chosen my college on the advice of a stranger on a bus and followed another stranger to a hotel. I had never managed anyone. I could not make a spreadsheet to save my life. I had never done any outreach or community development besides my volunteer work.

But I was passionate. I was determined. I was going to get things done.

A Woman's Voice

I went back to my town, determined this time to end FGM entirely. If the men refused to talk to me, I would keep bothering them until they did.

The *morans,* our young men, were the ones I most needed to convince. They were the ones who would marry soon. They were the ones who would be most insistent that their brides had the cut. If I could convince them, the rest of the people would follow.

To get to the *morans,* though, I needed to talk to the elders. After I had run from the cut, I needed my grandfather's support, not only because he was my guardian but because the younger men would not dare defy him. His ruling as an elder would not be challenged. With his protection, I might hear my uncle grumble, but he would not dare hurt me.

In much the same way, if I could get the elders' permission to speak to the *morans,* people might judge me, they might call me *entapai,* but I would be allowed to be heard. The elders had authority in our community, and I needed the shelter of that authority.

I was showing respect by trying to get their permission, and I hoped that many of them still remembered my parents fondly. I went to them with my head bowed, humble, and asked gently for just the right to talk to the *morans*. The elders laughed at me at first. I was young and foolish, not even an adult woman, and I presumed to challenge centuries of tradition. They would wave me away and tell me to go back to my family.

But I did not give up. I went to them every day, interrupting their other business, a fly that would not stop buzzing around their heads.

I told them stories of young women who had gone to college, become businesspeople, doctors, and accountants in Nairobi or even Europe or the United States. I told them of the homes that the women's elders could buy with the money the women sent back, of the refrigerators, motorbikes, and televisions in those homes. These women married later, I said, but when they did, their children were healthy, strong, and rich. I could see from the elders' faces that they were tempted. Who doesn't want to brag about their successful young child sending back money for computers and cell phones?

But they told me they were not convinced. They told me that going to school and having a career was fine for some women, but we were Maasai. We valued different things: cattle, children, tradition. We were a minority even in our own country, so if we did not fight for our way of life, we would fade away. Sending girls away meant ending the things that made our lives special.

Still, even though the elders challenged every one of my arguments, I could tell that they were listening. A dowry can buy cattle once, but an educated child can keep buying cows for many years.

After many days, they said they would talk to the *morans*. They would not promise anything. They certainly would not argue my case with the young men. But if I would just leave them alone, they would give permission. I set up a meeting.

Finally, I thought, *I am getting somewhere. The* morans *are young, willing to change, and they will listen to me.* I was making real progress.

But when I went to that meeting, not a single *moran* showed up.

I could not do it as a woman on my own. I realized that no matter how good my arguments were, if the men would not listen, my knowledge was useless. Fortunately, I have never been afraid to ask for help when necessary. One of the things I most value about my culture is how we work together. People in other parts of the world, North Americans in particular, tell stories of a lone individual doing things on his or her own. A maverick willing to take on everyone else. We do not see things that way. We get things done through working together, through cooperation and consensus. I was determined to bring about change, to make a new life for girls, but I was not determined to go it alone.

I approached Douglas, the young man who had gone through Amref training at the same time I did. Like me, he had gone away to college in Nairobi. I went to the apartment where he was staying. Though it was in a slightly better neighborhood than where I lived—you did not have to hide your phone when you walked on the street—his room was as cramped and full of books as mine.

"Look at us," I said. "Two young scholars."

We talked about our schools, where to get decent milk in the city, and of course the traffic (everyone in Nairobi talks about the traffic).

"Help me host a meeting," I said. "With you there, they will at least show up."

I was prepared to ask him questions and talk him around to my point of view, but he agreed right away.

"On our next break," Douglas said, "we will go home together and host a meeting."

It should not have surprised me that he took no convincing. Like me, he was committed to education. We had trained together. He was one of the few people in my town who understood exactly how damaging FGM could be, and he also understood how tough it was to change centuries of tradition.

At the first meeting we cohosted, a few *morans* showed up. *It is a start,* I thought. Douglas gave some basic health information, and then he asked me to speak.

As soon as I stood up, every man other than Douglas left the room. *Some start,* I thought to myself.

We did not give up, though it was frustrating. We could host meetings only when both of us could make it home, and we were both supporting ourselves through school in Nairobi. Progress was slow.

Still, we kept working. Douglas met with people when he was home. "Come to the meetings," Douglas said, "and Nice will talk about health. She is in college. She has a job in Nairobi" (he neglected to tell them that I was a part-time trainee). "She has good information."

At the next meeting, three men were willing to stay and listen to me speak.

I did not talk about FGM. I talked about taking advantage of programs offered by Amref and other NGOs. I talked about measures we could take to clean our water. I talked about organizing clinics to make sure all our children were vaccinated.

More men started attending. It was only after many meetings, over many weekends and holidays, that I finally brought up FGM.

The *morans* had slowly come to realize that I had knowledge and could be trusted. Even then, I did not lecture. I asked the men questions. I had learned from my father to ask and let people come to their own conclusions.

"When you marry a wife, do you want her to enjoy sex with you?"

They shifted uncomfortably, not happy to be talking to a young woman about sex, but eventually, most of them agreed that they did want that. It is a mistake to say that Maasai men do not want to share sexual pleasure with women; it is just that when FGM was the standard, mutual pleasure was not an option.

"If your wife has the cut," I said, "what do you think she feels during sex?"

They shrugged. They knew already that women with the cut did not enjoy, and sometimes even suffered during, sex.

"If your wife enjoys sex with you, do you think she will be happier?"

They nodded.

"Would you rather live with a happy wife or with one who is always grumpy?"

They laughed, but I think they thought about it.

Slowly, I started to introduce some facts into the conversation. FGM was treated as a woman's matter. Young men did not know much, if anything, about the process. They had undergone male circumcision to become *morans*. It was painful, very painful, but they had been brave and stoic during the cut. Many assumed that what women went through was similar.

I talked about the blood, the risks of infection, and the many complications women could suffer after the cut. It was not like removing a piece of skin; it was removing the entire visible part of one of the body's organs. For male circumcision to be equivalent to

FGM, we would have to chop off a large part of the penis itself, not just the foreskin. The men squirmed. They would not make eye contact with me. But they listened.

"Do you want healthy children?"

They looked at me as if I was a crazy person: of course they wanted healthy children. It was only then that I told them FGM could harm fertility and make childbirth dangerous.

One by one, the *morans* changed their minds about FGM. No one wanted a wife who was permanently disabled by the cut. No one wanted their wives to dread the pain of sex. No one wanted to lose a child or a wife to pregnancy complications. The *morans* agreed that they wanted to work with me to end FGM in our town.

I am not going to pretend that everything went completely smoothly after that. Ending a practice that has been in a culture for hundreds of years is not going to happen overnight. But when the *morans* went to their fathers and said they wanted uncut wives, families began to respond. Women who hated what had been done to them finally had a way of protecting their daughters. Girls felt empowered to speak up for themselves and resist.

One by one, families agreed to end FGM. Girls were allowed to forgo the cut and stay in school. Men began marrying women who were whole. Even Buya, that sneaky little boy who had made me cry by stealing my lunch, came over to my side. His first marriage had been arranged by his father and his wife had the cut. When Buya took a second wife, he chose her himself, and he made sure she was a woman who had not suffered FGM.

We ended FGM in our village. It took over three years, it took working at home on every break from school, but Douglas and I did it. One of the reasons it worked was that the change was not imposed from outside; it was something that people had agreed on together. "Change is from the West," people say. They see many reforms as ways of destroying our cultural traditions, of trying to erase our identity and replace it with a foreign one. But this change came from us, so we were able to save our girls in our own way, without destroying who we were.

But I had not saved Soila. In two sisters' lives, FGM was a divide past which their lives changed forever. I was doing things no girl in our town had ever done: going to college, living in the big city on my own, working for a large NGO. Soila was back home with an unloving husband and several children. I had made a difference, but I had not saved my own sister.

"People are talking about you," she said to me one day.

"I'm sorry," I said. "I can stop."

She laughed. "No, it is good. They are talking about stopping the cut. They are just not hiding it."

"I wish..."

"No, Nice. I chose this. It is my path to follow."

And there are still girls following Soila's path throughout the country and throughout the world. The problem is bad in Kenya, even though the procedure is now illegal, but it is even worse in some other African countries. In Somalia and Djibouti, almost all girls suffer FGM. In other African countries, primarily those in central and northern Africa, the percentages are smaller, but they are still far too high. Girls in the Middle East, India, and as far away as Indonesia also go through the cut. The cultural reasons for FGM may differ, as do the mechanics of the cut, but the effect is always to hurt girls. It often leads to early marriage and always leads to female subjugation.

It is estimated that about two hundred million women worldwide have undergone some form of the procedure. To put that number in perspective, it is larger than the number of girls and women in the United States. It's almost as many girls and women as the number who live in the entirety of the European Union.

I had succeeded on a small scale, but I still had to convince the rest of the Maasai, and then the rest of Africa and the world. My work was only just beginning.

The Sun and the Moon

When the world was younger, the sun and the moon were married. They wandered through the plains in the heavens, the sun leading, the moon following. Once a month, the moon would grow tired, and the sun would carry her. After a few days, when she felt rested, the moon would walk again.

One day the moon disobeyed the sun, and he beat her. The moon fought back, and their battle grew fierce. He gave her a black eye and many bruises, and she bit and scratched his face in return.

When they had once again made peace, the sun was embarrassed. He had lost control of his wife and let a woman injure him.

"I will shine so hot," the sun said, "that no one can look at me."

So the sun glowed harder, and the people could not stare at him without losing their eyesight. Soon people forgot that his glow had ever been pale.

The moon glowed on gently, unembarrassed. She was a woman, and her injuries were no shame. Today you can still look up and see her black eye and pitted face. But no one can tell that the sun was hurt by a woman.

Opening and Closing

For too many women I knew, marriage and children meant a kind of death. My elder half sister married young and had several children; she would never do anything else. My younger half sister, Mary, avoided an arranged marriage but contracted malaria and died giving birth. Too many women died, like her, too young, of diseases that might have been prevented with better medical care. Too many were lost because of early marriage and early childbearing.

For Soila, the world was closing up. Her husband had begun drinking, a little at first, but then every day. When he drank, he hit Soila. For Maasai men, hitting your wife is considered reasonably normal. Men are the heads of their households, and they believe it is their right, even their obligation, to provide discipline. While I certainly do not support hitting one's wife, and I would never allow a man to hit me, for most Maasai men, it is not something they do to hurt and humiliate women. Their intention is to chastise, and it is a private matter. A man will take his wife away from the town and beat her where no one can see.

Soila's husband, on the other hand, hit her at home. He hit her in front of the children. He screamed, and in the tight quarters of a Maasai town, everyone knew exactly what he was doing. Soila could not look her neighbors in the eye.

It was more than just the humiliation. When a Maasai man hits his wife, he rarely tries to hurt her. He hits her in order to get her to obey, and he does not use his full strength. Soila's husband would hit her in a drunken rage. He left bruises and black eyes. This was not discipline; it was abuse.

Her sons saw everything. Soila's eldest son is a quiet boy, the kind who watches and thinks before he takes action. As he saw what was happening to his mother, that natural quietness grew into something more. He would answer questions with one word or not at all. He started disappearing for hours at a time, avoiding home. His grades suffered.

When I visited Soila, her husband left her alone, and she knew she was safe for a few nights. Soila did not complain, but I knew how much she was hurting—she herself but also on behalf of her boys. And I knew she was suffering all alone.

I could not stay there and help her. Her husband might have tolerated a visit for a few days, but he would never have allowed me to move in permanently.

I offered to move nearby and help after my graduation.

Soila shook her head. "You are going to get an education. You will work."

"I can find work here."

"Clean rooms at a hotel? Work at a lodge? You did not go to school for that."

"I can find something."

She stared at me hard. "Nice, I want you at school."

"I can help."

She was quiet for a long time, but finally she said, "What difference will it make?"

The defeat in her voice took my breath away. But she was right. Even if I was home, I did not have the power to do anything substantial. I was a woman—a girl, really, since I had never had the cut—and I had no authority over men. I was *entapai,* a pariah who would never get decent work in my own town.

I had only a part-time job. The money helped, but it was not nearly enough to support me in Nairobi and Soila and the boys back home. Without an independent income, Soila and her boys relied financially on the very man who was hurting them.

With each visit, I watched Soila grow more quiet. She looked at the ground more than she looked at my face. She was tired—understandable with three children and constant work—but it was more than that. She had lost her sense of joy. She smiled when she saw me, and she still took pride in her sons, but she rarely laughed anymore.

First Job

Amref offered me a limited contract for a full-time job when I was in my third year of college. I would spend several months in the field assisting with research into the lives of the locals: their health practices, their health needs, what resources were available to them, and what they needed going forward. Amref would use the information we compiled to work with the local people to improve their health care.

My boss, Ndwiga, told me that I was prepared. He had seen me work at my part-time job and knew I was ready. I was not so sure. I was still a college student and would have to take courses on-line while working full-time. I was a small-town girl. I was young. What did I know? I felt like an imposter, a child sent to do a woman's job. *Everyone is going to wake up,* I thought, *and realize I do not belong.*

My boss introduced me to a man I will call Samuel, the person who was going to be my supervisor. He was going to take me to my first fieldwork assignment in Kibwezi, a town about two and a half hours from my hometown by car. Kibwezi looks a lot like the area where I grew up, but it is not Maasai land. Most of the people are Kamba, an ethnic group that, until recently, was made up of hunters or long-distance traders. Samuel and a driver picked me up in a large SUV. Samuel was casual but well dressed, perfectly calm, and seemingly unaware that I was terrified.

As we drove to Kibwezi, I could not stop thinking about how to behave. He was much older than me, from a different ethnic group, and he had spent a lot of time in Nairobi. I had no idea what the rules were. Should I shake his hand? Should I talk to him? Should I talk to the driver? Was I talking too much? Was I dressed appropriately? Was he going to realize that I had no idea what I was doing?

He acted as though having a young woman in the car was normal. "We should stop at a store. Once we get to Kibwezi, there is no good place to buy what we need."

We need to buy things? I thought. Even if I had any money, I would not have known what to get.

At the store, whenever he picked something out, he asked if I wanted one as well. Soap? Roll-on deodorant? Skin lotion?

With every offer, I shook my head. Was buying things for your coworker normal? Should I buy him something?

Samuel bought food and drinks, and he kept offering. I started to get worried that I might offend him, so finally, I agreed to accept a soft drink.

He seemed satisfied, and we continued on our journey. I noticed him watching me in the rearview mirror.

We finally reached the office, and he introduced me to my coworkers.

Jane, the woman who ran the office, must have noticed my tight shoulders and stiff smile. "You are going to be fine," she said. "But if you have any problem at all, come to me. We have all been the new girl."

"Come on," Samuel said. "Let's go out to the pub for *nyama choma*."

I had never been to a pub before, but Kenyans love meat, and everyone loves *nyama choma*. Traditionally, it's grilled goat or beef served with *kachumbari*, a dish of chopped tomatoes and onions. It is a special-occasion food, a feast.

We ate, and I relaxed a bit. My colleagues were kind to me. The others had a couple of beers, but I did not drink. Samuel told me a bit about the town we were in, about the people we would meet and the problems we would address. *Maybe*, I thought, *I can handle this*. He paid for the food—his treat for the new staff member, he said.

In the restroom, Jane handed me her phone number. In case I needed anything, she said.

Afterward, the driver took me back to my hotel, and Samuel got out with us. As the driver was opening the door, he also gave me his phone number. Just in case, he said.

I thanked Samuel for welcoming me to my new job.

He got out of the car. "I will show you how to use the room key."

I was not relaxed anymore. "I am fine," I said. "Really."

He walked right by my side to my room.

When we reached the door, he blocked my way. "Come on, now," he said. "Aren't you going to invite me in?"

"I have to go to sleep," I said.

"After I bought you meat?" he said. "Come on." He leaned over me, and I could smell the beer on his breath. "Remember," he said, "I am your boss."

I ran.

I had no idea where to go in a town full of strangers, so I went back to the office. I called Jane. I was trembling, barely able to speak.

I did not tell her what had happened. "I cannot stay alone," I managed to say.

I do not know if she suspected Samuel. Maybe she had seen him behave the same way with other young women. Maybe she thought I was a small-town girl afraid to sleep in a hotel room by myself. She said, "Of course. Come and sleep at my house."

The next day, I went in to the office, hoping that the night's actions had been forgotten. Samuel saw me enter, but there was no greeting this time.

He gave me no training, and I did not know what I was supposed to do on the job. Day after day, I would go in to the office and ask what he wanted, and day after day, he had no assignments for me. He would not speak in more than the barest of grunts. I was wasting my time, not helping Amref, not helping anyone.

I did not know I could go for help with a sexual harassment problem. In fact, I was not sure that what Samuel had done was wrong. As far as I knew, men would demand sex from female employees as a matter of course. In my small town, girls gave in to men's demands. Maybe it was the same here, I thought. Maybe I was the one in the wrong. I did not complain, and I felt utterly useless.

One day I finally went up to the women in the office. "Show me what you are doing," I said. "Let me help."

They taught me how to do small tasks around the office: proofread documents, make copies, answer simple email questions. I read every word of our training manuals. At first, maybe my coworkers wanted to get me out of their hair, but when I showed that I was eager and efficient, they gave me more tasks. They showed me how to take the raw data people were bringing in from the field and enter it in the computer.

Then I started going into the field myself, observing my coworkers as they asked questions and interpreting the answers. I know I could have done more with some direction from Samuel, but I managed to learn by offering my help to the others and refusing to be useless.

I started making my own reports. Many locals spoke Kamba rather than Swahili, so I had to use a translator. But I felt as though the people and I were communicating, and I was learning. Even though we were not that far from my home, these people's lives and needs were quite different from the Maasai's.

When I handed Samuel my reports, he said they were terrible and threw them in the garbage.

I introduced myself to Victor, a doctor who worked with the Ministry of Health. He was not a local, but he had been working in Kibwezi for years, and he knew the people well. He taught me about the local Kamba customs and the health problems in the community. He even taught me a few words of Kamba.

I got to know people in the area, not just as interview subjects but as friends. They brought me mangoes. They gave me the nickname Mutano, which means "ever happy" in Kamba.

"You are a good woman, Nice," one woman said, "but you need a man. When my son comes back, you'll marry him."

Victor and I spent hours talking, usually about our work, but occasionally about ourselves. He brought me little presents like earrings, which I could not wear because I was allergic to the metal, or a small Bible. We were not dating, but it felt nice to be appreciated. I was not *entapai* to all men.

Life was wonderful outside the office, but Samuel was still throwing away my reports, still telling me I was doing a horrible job without offering guidance. I had made a few friends in the office, and they urged me to tell my superiors.

So I went to Ndwiga and told him what was happening. To my surprise, he did not tell me not to lead my boss on. He did not tell me I was being difficult. He just nodded and said he would talk to Samuel.

The next day at work, Samuel asked me into his office. He did not apologize, but he did not yell at me either. He walked me through how to properly do interviews, training sessions, and reports. After that, he would hand my reports back to me, marked up, to show me how to improve my work.

I am not sure what Ndwiga said to Samuel, but life in the office was different after that. Samuel did not smile or treat me as a friend, but he did not proposition me or treat me as a pariah either. I was able to get the work done. I finally felt that I was earning my salary.

Years later, I learned what sexual harassment was, and I also learned that it is something that Amref will not tolerate. If I had gone to them sooner, my first job would have progressed much more smoothly. The organization would have supported me. And over the years, Amref's policies have gotten even more stringent. If Samuel did today what he did then, I doubt he would have kept his job. I know he has since left the organization.

When I returned to Nairobi after that first assignment, I expected to never work with Amref again. I had approached my boss with a complaint. I knew that Samuel was not going to give me a good report.

The day after I returned, Ndwiga asked me into his office.

Don't cry, I told myself. *Stay professional. There will be other jobs.* I took a deep breath and walked in.

"We have another position you would be perfect for," he said. "You should apply."

I barely listened after that. I was not going to be fired. I might be allowed to continue my work. When I went home that night, I cried and laughed.

The job was project assistant focusing on water sanitation and body rights. I would be working on issues such as HIV, birth control, and, most important to me, FGM. In charge was Peter, the man who had seen me speaking to girls in my hometown years earlier and asked the elders to allow me to train with Amref. Somehow, he remembered the village girl who would not stop pestering her people.

There were multiple candidates for the job. I felt unqualified in a room full of college graduates and people with years of work in the field. To be honest, I was one of the least qualified people there. I had not even graduated from college yet.

First, we all answered a series of questions on the computer. Then each of us sat for a panel interview. At first my voice was quiet, but as we continued to speak, I could see the interviewers' faces relax. I talked about the slow process of convincing my people to give up FGM. I spoke about how I followed my father's example, always listening first, always asking questions. As I spoke, I could see that the interviewers were listening to me, and I grew more confident.

I was happy with my interview. During it, I was sweating so badly I was afraid to raise my arms, but afterward I was happy with how I did.

But after a week went by, and then two, and I hadn't heard anything, I began to think I would not get the job. I told myself that was fine. I could take the time to finish my degree. I told myself that there would be other job openings with Amref or another NGO. I told myself that I could go home and spend more time with my family. I almost managed to talk myself out of my disappointment.

Then, a month after the interview, I received the call. Amref was offering me a permanent job. I did not ask about salary. I did not negotiate any details. Honestly, I was so excited that I forgot to say thank you.

I called Soila and screamed and cried into the phone, and of course she did not understand a word. When I had calmed down enough, I told her the news.

"Mother and Father would be so proud," she said.

I started crying again, and I don't think I got a word out during the rest of the call.

Soila

I managed to see Soila when I could, and her marriage only seemed to be getting worse. The men in our family had noticed the beatings, and so had the neighbors.

The Maasai do not believe in divorce. Men might take second or third wives, but the marriage bond, and the bond it creates between families, is something that cannot be broken.

The Maasai do believe in helping families, and they do believe in working out problems through talking. I joke that Maasai men are lazy because they sit around talking together all day while the women work. Everyone tells this joke because it is true. But talking is how our community has managed to stay together peacefully for hundreds of years.

So a group of my relatives went to talk to Soila's husband.

Soila's husband offered them tea (prepared by Soila). The men praised his cows and his neat home (cleaned by Soila). When men talk, it takes a while to get to the point.

"What is this we hear about you beating Soila?" my grandfather finally said.

Soila's husband sighed. "It is the drink, not me."

"Maybe you can drink less, then."

He agreed. It did not take much for the men to reach an understanding; Soila's husband must have realized even before the talk that his behavior was wrong. He stopped drinking every day. When he drank, he drank less. When he hit Soila, he did it in private. I was not happy that he hit her, but his actions were considered acceptable.

The men in my family did not threaten him. They did not have to. He realized that his behavior was being judged. He felt the disapproval of my family and his own people. In a small community, the feeling of being judged is a powerful motivation.

But it did not take long for him to be drunk again, and when he was drunk, he was violent in public again.

So my male relatives talked to Soila's husband again.

"This needs to stop," my grandfather said. "You are disrespecting our family. You are bringing shame on yourself."

Soila's husband looked down at his feet. Once again, he agreed almost immediately. "I am listening," he said. "I am going to do better."

I walked with Soila while the men talked yet again.

"How are you doing?" I asked.

She sighed. "This is my life. It is not that it hurts so much. But the boys: they see everything. I cannot protect them."

"Let me come help. You are more important than school."

She stopped walking. Her hands were balled up into fists and she clenched her jaw. "Never."

"But the boys..."

"I said never," she spat. She closed her eyes and took a deep breath. Her body relaxed a little and she spoke quietly. "We have both worked for this, Nice. It is what Mother and Father wanted. Don't you dare drop out of college. It is my dream too."

I had to listen to her. I would keep going to school. But I was not about to allow her to give up either. "I will do it," I said, "but then I am going to help you."

She nodded and even laughed a bit. "Of course you are," she said. "I always knew you would."

When my male relatives went to talk to Soila's husband, I stood behind them, frowning at him. When I came to visit Soila after that, her husband did not bother to tell me to leave quickly. He turned his back when I showed up. I did not care. Who was he to think he could judge me?

At least I knew that he would not bother Soila while I was there. I could not say the same about Soila bothering me.

"Your skin looks ashy. Have you been using your lotion?" she asked.

"I ran out."

"Too busy to take care of yourself?" she asked.

"I am working a lot."

"More likely you keep forgetting. Your head is always somewhere else."

"I will try to be better," I said. She was right. I did still daydream too much.

"We will walk to town later and you will buy some lotion. It is not going to be my fault if your skin starts flaking off."

"You do not have to take care of me," I said.

"Of course I do. Everyone knows I have four children, Nice."

"I know you are secretly proud of me."

"Do not get a big head."

"But you are."

"Maybe a little." She laughed. "But you still need to learn to take care of yourself."

We did not have to talk. I still was not a good housekeeper, but we could work beside each other, and just sensing the other's presence nearby made the work easier. That and knowing that when the chores were done, I would be eating Soila's cooking.

"Are you eating well in Nairobi?" she asked as I was just about to taste her soup.

I paused with the spoon just below my mouth.

"Have you . . . added anything?" I asked.

When I first came home from working in Nairobi, my brothers and sisters cooked a goat. When we got to the soup, I tasted an unfamiliar herb.

"What's that taste?" I asked my brother.

"It is a special seasoning since you have been eating all that bad food in Nairobi," he said.

I noticed that the others were not eating much soup. It was sweet of them to save it for me, I thought.

That evening, that "special seasoning" gave me a terrible case of diarrhea. They had added herbs to my soup to clean out my insides.

I wondered how much Soila worried about me eating bad food.

She laughed. "You look like I am trying to feed you poison! It is just soup, Nice. Eat it. It is good for you."

The boys, eating their soup nearby, laughed as well. They knew all about what my siblings had done to me.

Time to change the subject. "What do you want me to bring back next time?" I asked them.

"Candy!" they shouted. I was not the only one in the family with a sweet tooth.

Soila rolled her eyes. "That kind of food will make you sick."

I winked at the boys. They knew I would bring them some anyway.

Unfortunately, because of my job and my last few classes at college, I made it home only every couple of months. I had bought Soila a used cell phone, and we went through our precious minutes quickly. The phone calls helped, but it was not like being home.

Never Cry Again

My colleagues had degrees and years of experience. Who was I, a small-town girl not even out of college, to presume to work with them? I was also the only Maasai working in my group, which did not help. Many of my colleagues knew people more qualified than I who wanted my job; some of my colleagues had even wanted my job for themselves.

I was a project officer, a big leap from my few months as an assistant. I was part of a push to improve water and sanitation access. Under the supervision of a project manager, I was supposed to implement the program, working with locals, the government, and donors to get the job done. I had to make sure that all the groups were kept informed and were working together smoothly.

We had weekly meetings where we would go around the table sharing the progress we were making. Colleagues would ask questions and critique one another's methods. Since we would often be working on different sides of the country, it was a good way to learn from one another and become better at our jobs.

When it was my turn to speak, the critiques would begin. Why had I not followed established protocol? Why had I not followed up on a difficult question? Why had I not done more research? Why was I not making more progress?

After every meeting, I would find a place to be alone and cry.

It was true that I was green, but the critiques felt less about the job I was doing and more about me personally.

I hid the crying, of course. I would smile when I passed my colleagues, asking about their work. But I must not have hidden my feelings as well as I thought, because Peter found me one day. "Do not worry, Nice," he said. "We all have some trouble adjusting. I have faith in you."

But no matter how hard I worked, no matter how seriously I took the critiques, I never seemed to get better in my coworkers' eyes. If I solved one problem, another took its place. My boss might have had faith in me, but I was losing faith in myself.

One morning, I sat at my desk, willing myself to go out and start working. I could not move. *Maybe they are right,* I thought. *Maybe I am not good enough for this job. Maybe I should quit.*

It would be easier, I thought, *if I just went home.*

I called Soila. "I am not good at this," I said. "I will never be good at this."

"Nice," she said, "get ahold of yourself. You cannot quit. If some people do not like you, let them not like you. No one said this would be easy. Quit feeling sorry for yourself."

She was right. I just needed a tough Maasai mother to set me straight. My job was not about me. It hurt when people criticized, but there were more important issues to deal with.

After the next meeting, I took Peter aside. We walked in a garden near Amref's headquarters. "People can say what they want," I told him. "They can hate me if they want. But I have work to do. I am never going to cry again."

And I didn't. I answered their harsh words with calm responses, and over time, the harshness faded. I still heard criticism, but it was constructive, not meant to hurt. Maybe my work got better. Maybe, once I had more confidence, my colleagues saw my resolve and backed down. I do not know the reason, but things improved. I even received a compliment now and then.

As the years went by, I moved up the ranks at Amref. When a job opened up, I transferred into a project working solely on FGM. I was proud of my work on other projects at Amref, but this was my passion. I started doing exactly what I had done at home. I went to communities. I asked questions. I listened. And once I knew the needs and concerns in a community, once I understood what would motivate people to change, I acted. I helped people want to change, and because they wanted it for themselves, it was a change that stuck.

Community by community, I made a difference. First a handful, then hundreds, and then thousands of girls escaped FGM. I wasn't the only person responsible for that change, of course, but I did my part. I grew more confident knowing that I was making a difference.

I tried to leave those days of tears behind me. I do not hold grudges. I invite people who speak against me to tea. I find out what they need and want. We all have the same goal—to make life better for people in Kenya—so it is easy to find some common ground.

Now some of my harshest critics are my strongest allies.

One Community at a Time

I spend much of my time traveling throughout Kenya, trying to make a difference one community at a time. FGM is an international problem, but the changes I make through my work happen locally. Wherever I go, when I visit a small town, a school, a religious institution, or another NGO, I try to follow my father's example. Before I give my opinion, before I do anything, I listen. That is the Maasai tradition.

Solutions imposed from the outside, without input from the community, are bound to fail. One of my colleagues talks about how Westerners show up in their matching T-shirts, do a bit of work, and fly home, confident that they have made a difference. In reality, he believes, they have succeeded only in making themselves feel good.

I understand his point, but unlike my colleague, I do not think those Westerners have failed. Every meeting is an opportunity. Maybe one of those people in their matching T-shirts will make a substantial financial donation and ask their friends and families to do the same. Maybe one will inspire a little girl to go to school. Maybe those people will feel so good about the work they have done in Kenya that they go home determined to make a difference in their own towns.

My colleague is right in his way, though: you cannot make lasting change by flying in and imposing ideas. You have to understand why a problem exists in a particular community before you can come up with a solution. In many Islamic communities, FGM is seen as a religious imperative, though many other Muslims challenge this view. In some communities, the cut is seen as a hygienic matter. In others, it is a way of controlling female sexuality. Even among Maasai communities, there are cultural differences.

Not only is FGM different everywhere, but other community concerns are different as well. Some communities need more education. Some worry about communicable diseases. Some need clean water. Working to solve these problems alongside ending FGM, often making ending FGM part of the solution, ensures community support for lasting change.

What had worked in my community, and the ideas we shared there, would not translate to other places. If I was going to make a difference, I would have to go in with open ears and heart.

The best way to understand what I do is to go through a typical day.

Recently, I went to visit a school about four hours outside Nairobi. It is in a poor area, mostly grassland, and most of the people are Maasai.

When I arrive, the older girls are making chapatis for lunch. I do not say anything, but that is a troubling sign. Why aren't the girls in class, like the boys? Why are they being trained in domestic duties rather than doing academic work?

I try to ask the girls about their lives. They are quiet. Some are resentful of being asked. It feels as if they are pulling away, ready to be grown-ups. Also troubling.

I notice there are a lot of younger girls at the school, but few over the age of twelve. There are plenty of boys of all ages.

As we talk, there are soccer games going on. A group from Kibera, a large slum in Nairobi, is visiting. There will be a coed game between the Kibera players and the oldest students later, but first there are boys' and girls' games. When the girls play, the boys ignore them. When the boys play, everyone cheers.

I speak to the adults I see: teachers in charge, a group of Europeans volunteering at the school, and a couple of local parents. Their perspectives are all a little different, but I hear similar stories. Many of these girls are still getting the cut, even though it is illegal in Kenya. Many are getting married and dropping out of school. Those who are not getting married are getting pregnant at high rates. About 40 percent of the girls here have their first children as teenagers.

I ask these adults, "Why? What are these girls doing?"

They get boyfriends, the teachers say, and that gives them status. They feel like grown-ups.

"They go to overnight revivals at the church next door," the headmistress says. "And then they sneak away to have sex."

"Many of them live with distant relatives while they attend school, and older men in their own families are abusing them," say the European volunteers.

Everyone's opinion is most likely at least partially correct. Any solution to FGM in this community is going to have to incorporate all of these contributing factors.

A fifteen-year-old girl comes to the school for a visit. I will call her Sarah. We sit together in a room with her former teacher, her mother, and a Western donor to the school. Sarah has one child tied to her front in a sling. Another girl, a toddler, follows at her heels.

"I dreamed about her going to school," Sarah's mother says. "I wanted so much more for her than this."

Sarah says nothing.

"What a beautiful little one," says the Western donor. She picks up the baby and coos at her. The donor met Sarah several years ago, when she was an eager young student. Now Sarah does not talk above a whisper, and she sits with her head bowed. "Sarah, do you want to come back to school?" asks the Western donor.

The girl nods. The teachers agree to work with the girl, but it is unlikely she will finish her education. Her father married her young to get a dowry. Her husband wants her home to work and raise the children. The mother might support education, but the men will not. Without their support, the girl is powerless.

Sarah's little sister comes in. She smiles and laughs and weaves around our chairs.

"A few years ago," the teacher said, "Sarah was just like her."

It is hard to imagine the beaten-down teenager in front of me as vivacious and happy. But I have seen the same thing thousands of times.

Her old teacher puts her hand on Sarah's knee. "All we can do is try, darling."

I talk to a group of girls, young people just starting adolescence. They are shy, so I lead them in a song. We sing together in harmony, something that we as Maasai have been taught since we were babies. They relax a little.

"What do you want to be when you grow up?" I ask.

A few girls shrug.

"A teacher," one says finally, and a couple of others chime in.

"I'm going to Nairobi to drive a big *matatu*," says one. The other girls laugh.

"If you have a baby," I say, "can you do any of those things?"

They shake their heads. We talk on. I ask about their views on marriage, on FGM, on boys.

"Someone has a boyfriend," one girl says, staring at her friend. The other girls laugh. I laugh with them, but I cringe inside.

I ask about their least favorite subjects and their favorite music. We feel one another out, learning to trust, learning to work together.

I will not change anyone's mind that day. I do not expect to. It will be the first of many visits. In time, I will learn the area's problems and concerns. I will learn which people are the most influential. I will learn what tactics will most likely lead to change. Only then, with all the information, will I recommend a plan, and even then the plan will not be just mine. I will change it multiple times after input from all the locals. It will become our plan, our voice—not mine. That's why, even though FGM is illegal in Kenya, I will not call the authorities about Sarah, the fifteen-year-old with two babies. Law enforcement just drives the problem underground. When people are afraid of being arrested, they will continue to engage in FGM, but they will be more likely to lie about it, and less likely to cooperate with me. It is only when people are cooperating of their own volition, when they are fighting FGM because they think it is the right thing to do, that we can begin to make change.

Before I leave, I watch a little bit of the final game between the Kibera team and the locals. The Kibera players are both male and female, and they are brilliant. The local boys hold their own, but there is never any real contest. It is good to see the boys and girls from Kibera playing together. I notice that everyone cheers for the players equally. There are plenty of troubling signs in the community, it is true, but there are also signs, like this, of hope.

Changing Tradition

FGM is tremendously painful and tremendously damaging, but it is also often one of the highlights of a Maasai girl's life. I do not mean that she enjoys the cut or its impact; every girl dreads that. But she gets new clothes. She gets special instruction from the women who love her. Her family and friends roast meat and sing songs just for her. She gets to feel like a grown-up. For a Maasai girl, it may be the one moment in her life when she is treated like someone special.

It is not just the girls who value the ceremony. It is an opportunity for the entire community to celebrate. For the women, it is a break from the drudgery of daily life, a time to socialize with other women. For the men, it is a time to sing, eat, and drink with family and friends. For everyone, it is a way to gather as a community and mark a passage in our lives. It is the equivalent of a wedding, a bat mitzvah, or a quinceañera, a time to acknowledge a girl coming to womanhood, but also a time for the entire community to come together.

FGM needs to disappear. But the girl still deserves a special ceremony in her life, and the community still deserves a celebration.

We do not ask communities to give up their traditions. We ask them to replace the traditions with what we call Alternative Rites of Passage.

The Samburu people, neighbors of the Maasai who share a very similar language and culture, worked alongside Amref to develop Alternative Rites of Passage. The entire community, including church leaders, elders, and, most importantly, the girls themselves, created the rites as a way of discouraging child marriage while still honoring our traditions. The Maasai further developed Alternative Rites of Passage to better suit our own community. Part of my work with Amref has been organizing these rites in communities and working with the local people to adapt them to their own needs. Amref stays flexible; the beauty of Alternative Rites of Passage is that each community makes them its own.

My first Alternative Rites of Passage was in Noomayianat. Like that terrible morning when I first saw the cut, it was a community celebration, but for these festivities, we changed the focus to celebrating girls and their future accomplishments. For three days, girls received special instruction from older women, but in these lessons they learned about birth control, educational and economic opportunities, and personal health, not just about taking care of a husband and children. I did not have to hide with the girls under a tree outside of town when I spoke to them about the dangers of the cut and the opportunities they could have if they avoided it. The other teachers and I spoke with the blessing of the girls' mothers and grandmothers. Community women taught the girls about Maasai traditions, such as singing, bead making, and clothing.

Even the boys got lessons. Kenyan boys need to know about education and health as well, for both themselves and the girls in their lives. They need to learn that FGM is not just a girl's problem.

It affects the entire community, including the boys' sisters and future wives.

We ended the Alternative Rites of Passage with a candlelight ceremony. The girls had developed this part of the rites on their own; they wanted something that was about just them. The girls got beautiful, traditional clothes, just as they would have if they were undergoing the cut, and they walked in front of the community, each girl holding a candle, singing about extinguishing FGM and replacing it with the light of education. As I watched their faces pass, each lit by pride and candlelight, I smiled. Here was hope. Here was the future.

The entire community came together. Best of all, since the girls were not getting the cut, even a small, ceremonial one, they could join in the songs, dancing, and feasting that followed the ceremony. We did not destroy Maasai tradition. We honored it and made it better.

I have proudly attended dozens of Alternative Rites of Passage since that first one. I have watched girls with their heads held high singing about growing up and getting an education. I have watched quiet girls learn to project their voices and make speeches. I have watched their entire communities—men and women both—cheering them on. It makes me proud of my work, and it makes me proud to be a Maasai. I do not pretend that Alternative Rites of Passage solve the problem of FGM. Some of the girls who go through the ceremony end up having the cut later. But it is part of our arsenal, and it does help many girls avoid the cut. If I had been offered Alternative Rites of Passage, I might never have had to run.

I wonder sometimes what my parents would think of my work. Both believed in the Maasai, and they loved our people. They supported tradition, and our traditions included FGM. It was my mother, after all, who first took me to see the cut.

But both of my parents also believed in growing as a people and moving forward. For my father, that meant forming our own game reserves, taking a place in the Kenyan government, and, most of all, promoting education. For my mother, that meant farming and supporting women. I like to think that they began a process of growth, and that I am finishing it. I support what it means to be Maasai, but I am doing it without hurting girls. I hope that, were my parents here, I would be able to convince them, just as I have convinced thousands of others. I hope that they might even learn to be proud of me.

Ambassador

I had vowed to my boss, Peter, that work would never make me cry again, and I kept my word. I still listened to others, including their words of criticism, but I did not let their words hurt me.

Peter watched me progress from a small-town girl talking to a handful of girls about FGM to someone who could speak to hundreds at a time. I graduated from college and began working my way up through the ranks at Amref. I went into communities, often not Maasai, and spoke to elders, government officials, preachers, teachers, parents, and of course girls. Sometimes I had to take a few breaths and whisper encouragement to myself, but I always managed to speak.

Eventually, I helped save seventeen thousand girls from FGM.

Peter stopped by my desk one day and asked me to walk with him.

"Amref wants to end FGM by the year twenty thirty. I would like you to do more."

I was already working from dawn to well past dark every day, often on weekends. I managed to return home every few weeks, but usually only because I squeezed the trip into my work travels. I did not have any more time to give.

"Are you unhappy with my work?" I asked Peter.

"No, of course not. But I see you in a different role."

"I like my role now," I said. And I did. I loved talking with people. I loved seeing the hope on the faces of girls who spoke before the community, vowing to never get the cut.

"We want you to be a global ambassador," he said.

I laughed. I had never left Kenya. How could I be a global anything?

"You are the girl who ran from the cut."

"I don't understand."

"Nice," he said, "if I tell someone that thousands of girls get the cut, they will say that it is a terrible thing. But they do not really understand. If I tell them about the Maasai girl who ran from the cut, who hid in a tree, who escaped, I am telling them a story. I am making them feel. Facts do not change hearts and minds; feelings do."

"I cannot give speeches."

Peter shook his head. "I have watched you speak about FGM. Many times. You do not have to give a speech. Just tell your story. You have made a real difference here, but we need people in the rest of the world to care about FGM. We need them to pressure their governments. We need their money."

That night I called Soila. "Is this something I can do?" I asked her.

She sighed. "You have been doing this all along. Go talk to the world."

I accepted the offer.

First Speech

One of my first assignments as a global ambassador was to give a TED Talk in the Netherlands. They wanted me to share my story, how I had run away from FGM and then dedicated my life to helping other girls avoid the cut.

I was honored and absolutely terrified. I had no idea how to give an inspirational speech. I had never been outside Kenya. I had never even been on an airplane.

Frequent travelers take security checks, getting to the right gate, and boarding procedures in stride. I knew how to do none of that.

An Amref driver took me to the airport. We arrived at a tiny building, and security officers ran mirrors under the car. I had to step out and hand over my luggage. Guards opened my bag and rifled through it. Then I got back into the car, and we drove about a half mile to the airport itself. There more security guards waited, more questions. I worried that I would do something wrong, that I would not make it through.

Somehow, I passed through security and made it to my gate

(after reading each sign multiple times and asking several people for directions).

After I boarded the plane and took my seat, it hit me. I had been so busy worrying about getting to the plane that I had forgotten to worry about the flight. I gripped each armrest tightly as we took off, but it was not as frightening as I had thought. Once we were in the air, aside from hearing a slight rumble, I might not have known that we were in a metal tube in the air traveling a few hundred miles an hour.

Then disaster struck. I had to go to the bathroom.

Honestly, I was so green I was not sure that the plane even had a bathroom. How would that work thousands of feet in the air? But I watched a few people get out of their seats and go behind a tiny accordion door marked with figures of men and women, so I figured I would follow their lead.

Once I got in there, it seemed pretty self-explanatory, and I was relieved to find that something about traveling was easy.

Then I flushed the toilet, and I thought I had broken the plane.

In that tiny room, that flush seemed like one of the loudest sounds in the world. Surely everyone had heard and knew I had done something horrible.

I stood in the cramped space, unsure of what to do, for at least half an hour. I am not exaggerating.

When I finally opened the door, people were reading their magazines, watching movies, drinking water as if Armageddon had not just occurred in the tiny cubicle.

The noise had been completely normal, I realized.

Relieved, I decided to go back to my seat.

It was then that I realized airline seats all look alike. And that I had been so nervous about finding the restroom that I had forgotten to pay attention to how to get back.

So I walked up and down the aisle for another ten minutes, pretending to stretch my legs, looking for my empty seat. When I finally spotted my bag under one of the footrests, I promised myself that I would never leave an airline seat again without first marking it with a scarf.

When we landed, I wanted to kiss the ground with relief. Amref employees met me at the airport, so the trip from the plane into the city of Amsterdam was easy.

Everything about the country was strange. Back in Kenya, I sometimes felt chilly late at night or during the rain. In the Netherlands, I realized that I had no real experience with the cold. I slept in my bed away from home fully clothed, wearing my socks, under the covers, and I still was chilly. The tea was weak and watery. I had never tasted a sandwich before; cold food was something new to me. After taking a bite, I decided I had not been missing anything.

I wondered about my father on his one trip out of Kenya. Had he felt this way in London? How did he stay warm? We had missed him, but maybe he had missed us more.

But I met my dear friend Linda in Amsterdam, and she was as warm as the weather was dreary. She welcomed me into her home even though I was a virtual stranger. Her kindness made up for a lot of my homesickness.

I went through two days of intensive training. I learned how to stand, to project my voice, to maintain a nice tempo. I practiced the speech, which had been written by my Amref colleagues, dozens of times. It was a good speech, well researched and well written, but it was someone else's words. It felt unnatural, and no matter how much I practiced, I felt stiff reciting it.

Like my father, I sometimes had a heavy tongue; inspirational speaking was not my strength. I was worried that if I was tired or hungry, I would trip over my words. I had spoken in front of groups before, but never to a foreign audience, and never with my voice being streamed all over the world. Anyone with a computer could watch me. I swallowed hard.

The night before my speech, I learned that one of my uncles had died. Not through a phone call or a text, but through a post on Facebook. I had been trying to distract myself by mindlessly scrolling through social media, and there it was. I was shivering in a home in Amsterdam, and he was gone. It did not seem real.

After learning that news, I felt even more out of place. I felt like an imposter in a foreign world. I tried to smile and seem excited about my speech, but all evening my coworkers kept asking me what was wrong.

"This might be a horrible mistake," I said at last.

With Dirkje at my side, I called Peter back in Kenya. "I cannot do this," I said. I was breathing fast, and my words came out too quickly. I am amazed he could even understand me over our scratchy Wi-Fi phone connection.

"Is this the strong girl who said she would never cry again?" he said. "Show me that strong girl."

I laughed a bit but still felt as though I might start crying.

"Nice," he said, "I know how important this cause is to you. I know how much you care about the girls. I know you can do it. But you do not have to do anything you do not want to do. The choice is yours."

I took a deep breath. He had faith in me. I needed to be strong. "I will do it," I said. "But I want to use my own voice."

Dirkje and I worked together late into the night. I told my story simply and clearly, in my own words. I made a few notes on index cards. I practiced in front of Dirkje and my colleagues, but I turned my back so it felt as if it was just me and my story. Those words, my own words, felt right in a way that the elegantly written speech never had.

The next morning, I wore a beautiful Maasai dress and a necklace made by Aunty Grace. She had handed it to me before I left for the airport. "For good luck," she had said, "a piece of home." I touched the necklace to give me strength.

I was also wearing high heels. "Are you sure you don't want to put on something more comfortable?" asked Dirkje, always the practical Dutchwoman.

"No," I said. "I want to be above everyone."

Dirkje smiled and handed me a cup of hot cocoa, and something about the warmth flowing through my body calmed me.

On the way to the auditorium, she held my hand. I felt stronger with a caring person beside me.

I walked to the stage. I thought about the girls back home. I thought about what I had escaped. I thought about Soila.

I told my story. People said I did well, though I do not remember much of my speech.

When I got off the stage, Dirkje and my coworkers were crying.

There had been a standing ovation, so I was shocked. "What went wrong?" I asked.

"Wrong?" said Dirkje. "Nothing. That was beautiful."

The Maasai cry only when they are in distress, and even then we try to hide our tears. I learned later that the Dutch cry when they are sad, but also when they are happy, when they are laughing, when they are frustrated... for any reason at all, it seems, including when they love a speech.

Peter saw the speech streamed over the internet and called to congratulate me. People all over the world heard my story. I made FGM personal, and people listened. Peter was right. Facts and figures do not change hearts. But a story, simply told, about a fellow human does.

Black Stick

Maasai leaders from all our communities gather periodically at the base of Mount Kilimanjaro, as they have for generations. The mountain sits just over the border in Tanzania. The Maasai are divided between different countries, but the mountain watches over all of us.

For generations, the men had been meeting at the same spot, one that was special, almost sacred, to Maasai men. No outsiders were allowed to attend. Women were not welcome; in fact, the men kept the exact location of their meeting place a secret.

Things had changed, though. Maasai leaders had begun to work with Amref on a number of issues: clean water, preventive medical care, and of course FGM. For the first time, outsiders were allowed to attend as elders debated the Maasai constitution.

A few women came with Amref, but we were not allowed to go to the actual meeting place, and we waited in the nearest town. Our male colleagues would have to brief us when they came back.

The men discussed health issues and consulted experts from

Amref. When it came time to talk about some important health matters—prenatal care, infant mortality, childhood illness, and FGM—our male colleagues took a risk. "These are women's issues," they said. "We should listen to the women."

I was not there when the elders decided. I can imagine that the decision was not a quick one. The elders had already made a huge concession by inviting outsiders to the meeting; inviting women was an almost unimaginable innovation. But our men decided to trust Amref. For the first time in the history of the Maasai, they allowed women to have a voice. Along with three other female coworkers, I was invited to speak.

The leaders knew that we, as a community, needed to take a position on FGM. The cut had always been a part of our identity, but largely because of Amref, voices within the Maasai community had come to challenge the practice. It was time to take a position in our constitution. If the Maasai were going to continue to practice FGM, if it was going to be central to our identity, they were going to proclaim that. If it was time for innovation, and we were going to adopt new traditions, then they would proclaim that instead. Either way, the men were going to arrive at a consensus about what it meant to be Maasai.

I had rejected FGM, and I was Maasai. They wanted to hear what I represented. A young woman, an *entapai,* I was going to speak in front of our male leaders. My heavy tongue felt leaden in my mouth. I was dizzy, shaking. I did not know if I could do it. But I was determined to try.

Mount Kilimanjaro was there looking down on me. The mountain is visible over my hometown. At the meeting in Tanzania, it loomed. The council is a group of elderly men, each old enough to be my father or grandfather. They sat outdoors, in a semicircle, and

I stood before them. They looked enormous sitting there dressed in their finest clothes. I felt tiny.

I was trembling inside. I wanted to run away. I wanted to be anywhere but there. But I had to take action. I took a deep breath, asked God for help, and began to speak.

We are Maasai, I told the men, and our traditions matter. But we are also wise enough to change when it is necessary. FGM is harmful and dangerous, but that is not the only reason we should end it. In the modern world, we need education. We need mothers who can read to their children. We need men who establish careers before having families. We are a people who raise cattle. We are a people who love children. I do not want to change that. What I do want to do is abolish a practice that is holding us back. Women who do not get the cut marry later and are better educated. Men who are not taking care of a family too young have better jobs. Getting rid of the cut does not end our identity as Maasai. It makes us stronger, healthier, wealthier, so that we can be a great people going into the twenty-first century.

I saw the men begin to nod, and my voice got stronger. I could see the agreement on many of their faces.

They heard other speakers that day. And, being Maasai men, they debated for hours.

At that council, they changed the Maasai constitution to reflect our commitment to end FGM.

Later, they awarded me the Black Talking Stick. It is a symbol of leadership and strength. I do not think any other woman has ever received one. As I took it, I did cry a bit. I knew my mother and father would be proud. I had fulfilled the dream of helping our people that they had set in motion years before. I was no longer an outcast. I was officially a leader.

Bringing Soila Home

I was no longer an *entapai*. When I returned home, people would greet me, welcome me to their homes, take the time to talk and joke. Not everyone, of course: the uncle who took our money still barely speaks to me. But even some of the people who had hurt me, like my grandfather's wife, welcomed me home. We are even friends now. Life is hard enough without making it harder by bearing grudges.

I was not satisfied, though. I had saved thousands of girls, but I still had to save Soila. She had sacrificed for me; it was time to pay her back.

The next time my male family members went to speak with Soila's husband, I came along. I expect they thought I would sit in the back and quietly listen. If they thought that, they had not been paying attention.

"You have to stop hurting Soila," my male relatives said.

"I know," her husband said. "I need to stop the drinking. That is what makes me do it."

"Enough," I said. I did not scream. I did not make a scene.

But I spoke firmly, with authority. "No one is going to hit Soila ever again."

"Yes, yes. It will never happen again," said her husband.

"No," I said. "Enough. You have made promises before. Now we are done. She is leaving. She is taking her children. She is never coming back."

I expected him to walk out or stay and fight. I expected my family to argue. I was prepared for anything. I was going to do whatever it took.

I was not prepared for his answer. "Fine. She is in your hands now."

And just like that, after years of abuse, Soila was free.

I had enough money from my job to build a small home for Soila and the children in Kimana. It is not large, but it is clean, modern, and comfortable. Most of all, it is safe.

I bought land, and she started a small farm, just as our mother had. She grows onions, greens, and tomatoes, and she sells them to local lodges. It is no more than a couple of acres, but it is good black soil. A pump brings water to a small cistern, so the crops can grow even in the dry season. Small farms just like hers stretch along the riverside. She even employs a few men to help her run it; I think she enjoys bossing them around.

After a few months, she walked with a straighter back. She even looked younger. Her eldest son was not so withdrawn, and his grades improved. He was admitted to a boarding school in Nairobi, and he is doing well. Her middle son followed, and we expect the youngest to enroll next. All Soila's boys are going to go to college. She and I will make sure of that.

She is still the strict mother, and I am still the doting aunt. She tells her children that they better bring home good grades, and I hug them and tell them how proud I am of their accomplishments.

When I am home, I stay with Soila, and when she is in Nairobi, she and the boys stay with me. Soila and I speak to each other on our cell phones several times a day. I could not save her from the cut, but we have built a life together, and it is a good one.

A few months ago, Soila came to me, a huge smile on her face.

"Guess what I did," she said.

"Bought a cow? Got a good price for your tomatoes? Met a handsome man?"

She shook her head with each guess, and her smile got bigger. "Better," she said, and she slowly rolled up her sleeve.

On her arm was a tattoo with her sons' names. "People are going to think I am crazy," she whispered. Maasai women do not go to tattoo parlors. We both started laughing.

"People already think we are both crazy," I said. "We might as well have fun."

I went on to help many more girls by spreading the word about FGM worldwide. My TED Talk in Amsterdam was the first of many speeches. I have traveled throughout Africa, Europe, North America, and Asia. Each time I speak, I drink a cup of cocoa, and I feel the calm wash over me the way it did when I accepted a cup from Dirkje before my first speech. And even if Dirkje would shake her head at their impracticality, I always wear gorgeous stiletto heels. It is part of a routine I have developed to help my tongue feel a little less heavy. I am proud to know that my work has helped raise awareness and bring in millions of dollars to fight FGM.

A few years ago, my boss at Amref offered me a job in upper management. I would have made more money and had more authority. I turned him down. I am not meant to sit at a desk and oversee other workers. My job is to get out into the community and help with my hands.

Instead, I chose to build A Nice Place on land once owned by my father. It opens officially on October 10, 2021, the International Day of the Girl Child. A Nice Place will be a safe haven for girls fleeing FGM. It will be the kind of place I needed when I fled from the cut years ago. Under our watch, girls will be free to grow and learn without the fear of their families forcing them into early marriage.

It will also be a place for young women to learn to shape their worlds. When I was growing up, there were no female leaders. No, that is not entirely true. There were women like my mother, who introduced farming and merry-go-rounds to our community to help women. But no one encouraged girls to take leadership roles and to make positive change in the world.

I am making it my mission to create a generation of female leaders. A Nice Place is going to be a facility where girls from Kenya and Tanzania can come for training. We are building a clean, simple, solid building. There will be modern plumbing and a modern kitchen and room to do our work. Girls will learn practical, marketable skills. I have noticed in my travels that Westerners like their jewelry simpler and less colorful than we do; instead of necklaces that are a riot of color, they like one or two colors at the most. The girls will learn to make those. Once they have the skills to cater to Western tastes, they can bring more money home.

But much more importantly, A Nice Place will teach leadership. It will teach girls to change their communities. It will empower girls to take charge. I turned down a management position to keep working in our communities because change is best achieved person-to-person.

The problem is, one person can only reach so far. When my father died, there was no one to replace him, and many of his reforms, including the game reserve he had worked so hard for, fell apart. The land is still there, but there is no one to operate it. That is not going to happen when I am gone because I am going to leave hundreds of people to do my work. A Nice Place will help build an army of strong, knowledgeable girls, spreading out through the Maasai lands in Kenya and Tanzania. Each of those girls will, in turn, inspire other girls to follow her. Female leadership will spread like a virus—a good virus—and the work will spread. Someday maybe we will send girls throughout Africa and even the rest of the globe. We are going to change the world.

Years ago, I changed my life by running from the cut. I ran farther than I could have ever dreamed. I am still running. I am going to keep going until every girl in the world can live her life to the fullest. I am going to run until all my dreams come true.

Acknowledgments

I would not be the woman I am today without the love and support of so many people in my life.

I was blessed to be born in a beautiful village in Kenya where I could wake up in the morning and see Mount Kilimanjaro in Tanzania. This is where my dreams began, nurtured by my family.

I owe gratitude to my Maasai community for taking this journey with me and courageously choosing to make a needed change.

To my dear friends from all walks of life who have been with me every step of the way, sharing the joys and the difficult times: I sincerely and deeply thank you.

To my Amref Kenya family, and my Amref family worldwide, past and present: You have been an important part of my journey, and you have been my other home. You welcomed me to Canada, Ethiopia, France, Germany, Italy, the Netherlands, Senegal, Spain, Tanzania, the United Kingdom, and the United States of America and taught me how to be comfortable in advocating for the rights of women and girls and bringing the much needed change in the quest to end FGM. I owe much gratitude to Dr. Githinji Gitahi, Amref Health Africa Group CEO, for the mentorship and guidance during this journey.

I want to give special thanks to everyone who has been involved with the writing and publication of this book, helping me to share my experience and my passion for the rights of girls and women. My agent, Peter McGuigan, helped bring the dream to reality. Elizabeth Butler-Witter helped put my thoughts into words. I'd like to thank Judith Clain, Miya Kumangai, Ben Allen, Heather Boaz, and all the employees of Hachette Book Group. And, of course, Norm Aladjem and Robert Kelty, who started me on the journey to this book. I would also like to thank Emmanuel Jambo, Giulio Paletta, Humberto Tan, Jeroen van Loon, Joost Bastmeijer, Luca Antonio Marino and La Fundación Princessa de Asturias for the use of their wonderful photographs in this book.

I would like to thank Neelie Kroes, Annemiek Hoogenboom, Katja Iversen, Emma Bonino, and all the Nice Foundation funders. And all the amazing girls and women I meet every day who are making immense change in this world and who continuously inspire me to keep going. Their courage and determination have been my greatest inspiration. Thank you also to Dr. Biko Yoni.

Finally, for bringing me into this world, I owe thanks and love to my late parents, Paul Leng'ete ole Nangoro and Alice Mantole Leng'ete. To my grandfather who brought me up to be the woman I am today, and my sisters, brothers, and nephews who kept the fire in me burning.

About the Authors

Nice Leng'ete is a human rights activist from Kimana, Kenya. When she was eight years old, she defied cultural convention and fled from female genital cutting. Nice is the first woman in Maasai history to be bestowed with the Black Talking Stick, known as *esiere*. The stick is a symbol of leadership and allows Nice to engage in conversations with men and the elders, a right usually denied to Maasai girls. Nice advocates to end female genital mutilation and replace it with Alternative Rites of Passage. Through her work with Amref Health Africa, she has helped save an estimated seventeen thousand girls from the cut and forced childhood marriages. Nice created A Nice Place, a leadership training academy and rescue center, which is a sanctuary for girls at risk for circumcision and early marriage, and a place for them to realize their full potential.

Elizabeth Butler-Witter lives in Decatur, Georgia. A former attorney, she now works to help people tell their stories. A mother of two, she feels privileged to work with women like Nice, who are making the world a better place for her children.